"DISHON(

The "Colonels' Surrender" at St. Quentin, The Retreat from Mons, August 1914

Peter T. Scott

Tom Donovan
London

First published in 1994 by
Tom Donovan Publishing Ltd.
52 Willow Road
Hampstead
London NW3 1TP

© Peter T. Scott 1994

ISBN: (hardback) 1-871085-24-1
ISBN: (paperback) 1-871085-25-X

Desk-top typeset in Palatino by Tom Donovan Publishing Ltd.

Printed by Antony Rowe Ltd., Chippenham

Contents

Maps

Acknowledgements

I would like to express my thanks to the following individuals and institutions for their assistance and permissions in the course of the research for this work: Army Historical Branch, Ministry of Defence; Martin V. Battey; Brigadier J.K. Chater, Regimental Area Secretary (Warwickshire), The Royal Regiment of Fusiliers; G. Christian; Commonwealth War Graves Commission (Miss Maria Choules, Enquiries Section); Jennifer Cranfield; M.J. Griffiths; Dr. T.A. Heathcote, Curator Sandhurst Collection, The Royal Military Academy Sandhurst; Dr. E.R.Holmes, OBE, TD, ADC, JP; Mrs M. Huckerby; Norman Hurst; Sue Hutchinson; Imperial War Museum (G. Clout, Department of Printed Books; Nigel Steel, Department of Documents); Tom Knott; Peter H. Liddle, Keeper Liddle Collection, Leeds University Library; Peter C. Metcalfe; J.A.L. Miller; National Army Museum; News International PLC (Eamon Dyas, Group Records Manager); J. Overett; Public Record Office; S. Roberts; Keith Simpson; Mrs A. Sutton; Penny Swannell; Jennifer Turner; Warwickshire Country Council (Gary Archer, Regional Information Officer); H.R. Yates; Andy Simpson.

Introduction

The basic facts of the attempted surrender by Lieut.-Colonel J.F. Elkington and Lieut.-Colonel A.E. Mainwaring at St. Quentin on 27th August 1914, their subsequent court martial and cashiering, and the rehabilitation of Elkington, have been known for many years, some details emerging before the end of the Great War.

The 1921 history of the Royal Warwickshire Regiment, whose First Battalion was one of those involved, made a brief reference to the events at St. Quentin. On the other hand the 1923 history of the Second Battalion Royal Dublin Fusiliers, the other battalion involved, carefully skirted the whole event, as had their Brigade Commander in his account published in 1920.[1]

The first eyewitness accounts appeared in the 1930s. That by Lieut.-Colonel Arthur Osburn, an onlooking cavalry medical officer at St. Quentin, was published in 1932, while that by Lieut.-General Sir Tom Bridges, the principal actor in frustrating the surrender, appeared in 1938. Oddly, the only published account by a participating private soldier, R.G. Hill, that appeared in 1930, made no mention of the attempted surrender.[2] The "two colonels" have also figured briefly in more recent studies, where their treatment has veered from the calamitously erroneous, via the vaguely misinterpreted, to the merely inadequate.[3]

The opening of public and private military archives over the past thirty years has revealed a substantial amount of material concerning the Retreat from Mons and this, taken together with the published sources, made it possible to reconstruct at least some of the events that befell the two sorely tried battalions during the Battle of Le Cateau and the various parties into which they fragmented during the Retreat. However, only with the discovery of a copy of the privately printed and circulated *Statement* by Lieut.-Colonel Mainwaring has it proved possible to prepare this narrative that, for the first time, includes the direct evidence of one of the "two colonels."

This is not, therefore, a history of the Retreat from Mons, or of the Battle of Le Cateau, but it is an account of a series of extraordinary incidents common to both and it is offered as a contribution to the history of both.

Peter T. Scott, September 1994

1
The Professionals

Neither before, nor since, has the British Army been better prepared for war than it was in August 1914. The reforms of Edward Cardwell and Hugh Childers in the nineteenth century, the practical though bitter lessons of the Boer War followed by the consolidating reforms of R.B. Haldane, had forged in the Regular Army a skilled, professional fighting force that, although small in comparison with the conscript armies of its continental neighbours, had as its backbone the self-sustaining vigour and discipline of a Regimental system without equal. Moreover, in the creation of the British Expeditionary Force (BEF) and arranging for its deployment to France, the subsequently much maligned staff had performed extraordinary feats of detailed planning, organisation and administration on a scale never previously attempted and seldom subsequently equalled.

The BEF comprised six infantry divisions and one cavalry division that, at War Establishment and together with all the necessary administrative arms and services, totalled some 128,000 officers and men. An infantry division had a War Establishment strength of 18,179 all ranks and comprised three infantry brigades, each four battalions strong, a Cavalry squadron, three field artillery brigades (54 18-pdrs.), one howitzer brigade (18 4.5-inch howitzers), one heavy battery (4 60-pdrs.), two Royal Engineer field companies, one Royal Engineer signal company, three field ambulances, four Army Service Corps horse transport companies, and one mobile veterinary section to attend to the division's 5,594 horses.

It cannot be emphasised enough that about one third of the War Establishment strength of a division and indeed the BEF as a whole was provided by the army's Regular Reservists. These were men who, having completed their sevice with the colours, had returned to civilian life on the understanding that they would return to their regiments when a General Mobilization was proclaimed. Immature, partially trained recruits and young soldiers below the age for active service (19 years) had to be left behind on embarkation and the army was therefore totally dependent on the Regular Reserve for the additional men to place it on a war footing.

The Fourth Division of the BEF was based in Eastern Command and since May 1911 it had been commanded by Major-General Thomas D'Oyly Snow, CB, age 56, whose headquarters were at Woolwich. Its infantry brigades were the 10th with its headquarters and three battalions at Shorncliffe Camp, near Folkestone, and a fourth at Gravesend, the 11th at Colchester, and the 12th with its headquarters and three battalions at Dover and a fourth at Chatham. (See Appendix I for the Fourth Division Order of Battle).

Snow's "gifts for training and command of troops were clearly manifested" as commander of the 4th Division. "He concentrated particular attention upon making junior officers criticize each other's work, on movement by night, on march discipline, then in its infancy, and on concealment from the air, an even younger matter, and produced a set of standing orders for war which were made use of by other divisions in the war 1914-1918."[1] This was the opinion of Br.-General Sir James E. Edmonds, the British official historian, who was Snow's senior staff officer (GSO1) at 4th Division from 1911. According to Captain Cyril Falls, another official historian, Snow was a "formidable and irascible man" who gave Edmonds "his complete confidence and at an early stage said to him 'I provide the ginger and you provide the brains'. This was very much to Edmond's taste, and if ever he spoke with excessive pride it was of his achievement in the training of the 4th Division for the war..."[2]

Snow thought himself "lucky in my staff" and considered Edmonds "a man with a brain and an education not often met with in a soldier... I cannot imagine a better staff officer or at any rate one who suited me better. He was not, however, over robust."[3]

To judge by the later careers of some of them Snow was indeed lucky in his staff. His GSO2 was Lieut.-Colonel A.A. Montgomery (later Field-Marshal Sir Archibald A. Montgomery-Massingberd), his DAA & QMG was Captain B.F. Burnett-Hitchcock (later Lieut.-General Basil F. Burnett-Hitchcock), his DAQMG was Captain H.J. Elles (later General Sir Hugh J. Elles), and his CRA Br.-General G.F. Milne (later Field-Marshal Lord Milne). See Appendix II for the Fourth Division Staff List.

In August 1914 Snow considered that his division could be "put down as having arrived at as high a state of efficiency as is possible in peace, but we were terribly short in numbers and the restrictions as to training ground cramped the important study of ground. Still the training of the officers had reached a high level and there were sufficient N.C.O.s and men trained to leaven the reservists when they arrived."[4] He thought his brigade commanders, Br.-General J.A.L. Haldane (10th Brigade), Br.-General A.G. Hunter-Weston (11th Brigade) and Br.-General H.F.M. Wilson (12th Brigade) "were far and away better than the Brigadiers of other Divisions and all became Corps Commanders. I knew their ways and they knew mine."[5]

They did indeed. In his diary Br.-General Haldane was vehemently critical of Snow, castigating him as "no tactician" and "Not in favour of bold methods."[6] Following a Command Staff Tour at Bedford in May 1913 Haldane wrote that his divisional commander "again showed his ignorance of any tactical principles, and had we not been fighting an imaginary enemy (territorial troops) we should certainly have been beaten; as it was the fight was considered drawn, whereas by massing against the enemy's nearest flank he could have been routed. General Snow ignored the principle of economy of force, of direction, the mass and security. He, however, was quite pleased with himself."[7]

Aylmer Haldane was 52 years old and had been commissioned in the Gordon Highlanders in September 1882. He was probably best known, both inside and outside the army, for his exploits during the Boer War and particularly for having been in command of the armoured train that was derailed by Boers between Chievely and Estcourt in Natal with the result that the party, which included Winston Churchill, fell into Boer hands. Haldane followed Churchill in escaping from imprisonment in the State Model Schools at Pretoria and, like Churchill, wrote a book about his experiences: *How We Escaped from Pretoria* (1900). From February 1904 to December 1905 he had served as Military Attaché with the Japanese army in Manchuria during the Russo-Japanese War and between October 1906 and September 1909 he had been Assistant Director of Military Operations at the War Office. He had succeeded Snow as Brigadier-General General Staff at Eastern Command headquarters in October 1909. In April 1912 he had taken command of the 10th Brigade that in August 1914 comprised 2nd Seaforth Highlanders, 1st Royal Irish Fusiliers, 2nd Royal Dublin Fusiliers and 1st Royal Warwickshire.

In marked contrast to Haldane's opinion of his GOC, Snow apparently held a high opinion of his subordinate. In his December 1913 confidential report Snow described him as "one of the most energetic officers both mentally and physically whom I have ever met.

He is a first class instructor in all stages of training, an excellent commander in the field with a quick eye for country and a situation, and can rapidly apply his deep study of military history to the task in hand.

He is very methodical and has had an unique experience in both the office and in the field.

He has the confidence of his subordinates and I am fortunate in having in him a brigade commander I can put absolute trust in both as regards loyalty and action."[8]

Glowing opinions were also expressed by others. General Sir Charles Douglas, the Inspector-General of the Home Forces, considered Haldane "a good instructor" who "had established a good system of training in his brigade" and who took "a great amount of pains and to produce satisfactory results... he promises to be a thoroughly efficient brigade commander."[9] Major-General Sir Archibald Murray, the Inspector of Infantry, believed Haldane's 10th Brigade and the 13th Brigade (commanded by Br.-General Thompson Capper; 5th Division in Ireland) to be "the best in the army."[10] Lieut.-General Sir James Grierson, GOC-in-C of Eastern Command and commander designate of the BEF's II Corps, concurred in these views. Haldane was "a first rate brigade commander, quick in his decisions and resolute in action, and he has brought his brigade to a high state of efficiency." [11]

Haldane modelled his style of command and system of effective tactical training based on "sound principles" on the work of Sir John Moore who, when he had commanded at Shorncliffe in the early 1800s, had introduced the system of drill, manoeuvre and discipline "that laid the foundations of the famous Peninsula light division."[12] Indeed, such was Haldane's fascination with Moore that throughout his command at Shorncliffe his spare time was largely taken up with raising funds towards erecting a statue and building a lecture hall and reference library in honour of his hero.

Haldane may indeed have enjoyed "the confidence of his subordinates," but his confidence in some of those subordinates was often less than wholehearted. His particular *bête noir* was Lieut.-Colonel D.W. Churcher, commanding the 1/R. Irish Fusiliers from September 1910. Haldane soon came to the conclusion that Churcher was quite useless:

"He has evidently allowed slackness in his battalion in spite of my warning when I first took command of the brigade and subsequently...

There is too much 'eyewash' about this battalion; they do not take interest in anything but sport and the C.O. is a humbug. As long as he is in command much improvement is impossible, but it is not easy to get rid of a C.O. in peace time."[13]

Despite Haldane's repeated warnings and strongly adverse confidential reports Churcher quite failed to take a grip on his battalion and his apparent indolence and hubris did not endear him to Haldane, nor did they bode well for his future, or that of his battalion.

Up to June 1913 the 2/Seaforth were commanded by Lieut.-Colonel Douglas Campbell who was then succeeded by Lieut.-Colonel Sir Evelyn Bradford, Bt. During the later stages of Campbell's command the battalion had suffered from a serious outbreak of drunken misconduct that had come to the notice of the King. Haldane considered that the Regimental Depot in Glasgow had been at fault in recruiting men of known bad character who, when they reached Shorncliffe, gave the battalion "a bad name which so fine a unit does not deserve, and which reflects on the C.O., who is a good commander."[14]

Under the new commander things improved markedly and by the time of Haldane's January 1914 confidential reports the 2/Seaforth were the only battalion of his brigade whose assessment did not include adverse comments on drunkeness, only that "More attention to be paid to march discipline."[15]

The 1/R. Warwickshire, commanded by Lieut.-Colonel H.R. Vaughan, had joined the brigade from India early in 1913 to replace the 2/King's Royal Rifle Corps. Haldane was soon of the opinion that "I shall have to teach the Warwicks everything as I don't think the C.O. is capable of doing so... Shall have to frighten Lt.-Col. Vaughan the C.O. as I had to do Churcher...".[16] Moreover, he took a dislike to the Warwickshire's mascot: "Had trooping the colour... Warwicks were very slow. I dislike their black buck which they have on ceremonial parades. To-day it had to be dragged past. Too much circus about it."[17]

Haldane was regularly out and about, often turning up unannounced, inspecting officers and men alike to ensure that they kept to his system of training. He seems to have had frequent occasion to make adverse comments on the officers of his command, as in this diary entry in October 1913:

"Saw Royal Warwicks doing bayonet-fighting and standard tests. Major Poole, the commander of the company, is slack. He was president of a court-martial and allowed his captain at the same time to go out hunting so that he was not with the company... Common sense or sense of duty should show officers the necessity for their being present, but they are far less well disciplined than the men, are careless in obeying and carrying out orders, and do not regard Individual Training seriously enough."[18]

We will meet Major A.J. Poole again.

On 24th February 1914 Lieut.-Colonel Vaughan handed over command of the battalion to Lieut.-Colonel J.F. Elkington.

John Ford Elkington was born in Newcastle, Jamaica, on 3rd February 1866, the first of the five sons of Major-General J.H.F. Elkington, CB (1830-1889). At the time of the birth his father was Senior Major of the 2nd Battalion 6th (Royal Warwickshire) Regiment of Foot, which had been stationed on the island since 1864.

Elkington senior had obtained an Ensigncy in the 6th Foot in 1846 and served in the Kaffir War of 1847, in the Crimea in 1855 and 1856 as AQMG to the Ottoman Contingent at Kertch, as ADC to General Sir John Michel in India during the mutiny of 1858 and as ADC to Major-General Sir (James) Hope Grant during the 1860 campaign in China where he was present at the capture of Peking.

The 2nd Battalion returned to Britain in 1867 and Elkington senior succeeded to its command in November of that year. For the ten years that the battalion was under his command it served at various home stations, including the Channel Islands, where his eldest son was educated at Elizabeth College, Guernsey. During an inspection in 1873 the Commander-in-Chief, the Duke of Cambridge, highly commended the "excellent battalion, so well commanded by Colonel Elkington."

John Ford Elkington attended the Royal Military College, Sandhurst, with an Honorary Queen's Cadetship between April 1885 and February 1886, when he obtained a commission as Lieutenant in the Royal Warwickshire Regiment. He went to the 1st Battalion, was promoted Captain in January 1893, embarked with them for Malta in November 1895 and accompanied then to Egypt in 1897. He returned to the Regimental Depot in March 1897 and remained at home until March 1899 when he was attached to the West African Frontier Force and served in Northern Nigeria until May 1900.

From June 1900 to August 1901 he served in South Africa with the 2nd Battalion and saw action during the Boer War at Belfast, Transvaal (Queen's Medal with 4 clasps); he was promoted Major in April 1901.

Between August 1901 and November 1902 he served with the 2nd Battalion in Bermuda, between November 1902 and April 1906 at home, and between April 1906 and February 1907 in South Africa, probably with the 3rd Battalion.

Elkington married Mary Rew, the daughter of John Rew of Liverpool, at Whitchurch, Oxfordshire, on 9th July 1908. Their first son, John David Rew Elkington, was born at Purley Hall, near Reading, on 25th July 1909, at which time his father was serving with the 1st Battalion at Peshawar.

Haldane's fourth battalion, the 2/R. Dublin Fusiliers, was stationed at Gravesend and he considered them to be of a similar quality to the three at Shorncliffe. However, he did note that they had particular problems with their Special Reserve officers: "One of them... hired a bicycle and pawned it."[19] The battalion had been commanded by Lieut.-Colonel A.E. Mainwaring since 5th March 1912.

Arthur Edward Mainwaring was born on 5th June 1864, the son of General W.G. Mainwaring, CIE, Bombay Staff Corps (1823-1905) who, at the time of the birth, was the Major commanding the 30th Native Infantry (Jacob's Rifles) at Jacobabad in the Upper Sind district of the Bombay Presidency. His service had commenced in 1843 with an Ensigncy in the Honourable East India Company's 1st Bombay (European) Regiment. The following year the regiment became the 1st Bombay (European) Fusiliers, in 1858 its title was changed to the 1st Bombay Fusiliers and in 1861 it became the 103rd Royal Bombay Fusiliers.

Mainwaring senior served with the regiment in the Punjab Campaign of 1848-49, with the expeditionary force in Persia in 1857 and in the Indian Mutiny, 1857-58. He commanded Jacob's Rifles in the Afghan War and took part in the Battle of Maiwand and the defence of Kandahar.

In 1881 the 102nd and 103rd Regiments were linked together as, respectively, the 1st and 2nd Battalions The Royal Dublin Fusiliers. So, when Mainwaring junior completed his Honorary Queen's India Cadetship at the Royal Military College in February 1885, it was natural that he should secure a commission as Lieutenant in the 2/R. Dublin Fusiliers, the direct successors of his father's old regiment who were then stationed in Egypt. He served with them there and in India and was promoted Captain in 1894. He was serving at the Regimental Depot at Naas, County Kildare, at the outbreak of the Boer War.

The battalion's service in the Boer War is described in detail in *The Second Battalion Royal Dublin Fusiliers in the South African War*, written jointly by Major C.F. Romer[20] and Mainwaring and published in 1908.[21] Their history is rather reticent on the subject of Mainwaring's Boer War service, but it does disclose that he joined the battalion at Dornbult (a halt on the Vryburg to Mafeking railway) on 31st May 1900, having arrived in South Africa a few days previously. His official, published war record is as follows:

> S. African War, 1899-1902 - On Staff. Operations in the Transvaal, west of Pretoria, July to 29 Nov. 00, including actions at Frederickstad (17 to 25 Oct.).
>
> Operations in the Transvaal 30 Nov. 00 to 31 May 02. Queen's medal with 3 clasps. King's medal with 2 clasps.

From the *Army List* it is possible to add that he served as a Press Censor in South Africa from 11th June 1901 to 30th June 1902. He therefore did not accompany the battalion when it embarked at the end of January 1902 for Aden where it served until October 1903 before returning to Ireland.

Between October 1902 and December 1903 Mainwaring served as Adjutant of the 3rd Battalion, The Kildare Militia, at Naas and then joined the 2nd Battalion at its new station at Buttevant, County Cork. He was promoted Major in July 1904 and Lieut.-Colonel in March 1912 on appointment as commanding officer of the 2/R. Dublin Fusiliers in succession to Lieut.-Colonel Walter Bromilow.

Mainwaring did not marry until June 1912, when he was 48. His bride was Clarice Hare, the 29 year old widow of Lieutenant Henry A. Hare, King's Own Yorkshire Light Infantry, who had died in 1907, aged 25.

Mainwaring's successful collaboration with Cecil Romer was not his first published work. The first edition of his handy guide *Cut Cavendish; or, Whist in a Few Whiffs (with a postscript on Bridge)* had appeared in 1899 and been followed by a new edition in 1905. In 1910 there had been two editions of his pocket guide *The ABC of Croquet* and 1912 had seen the publication of his *The Whist-Drive Manual*. However, his major work and his most lasting literary memorial, was *Crown and Company: The Historical Records of the 2nd Batt. Royal Dublin Fusiliers, formerly the 1st Bombay European Regiment, 1666-1911*, written and published when he was second-in-command of the battalion. It was greeted by Lieut.-Colonel Stuart Huntly Hooper, military correspondent of *The*

Times, in his anonymous review in *The Times Literary Supplement* as a work that "not only shows traces of deep and often wearisome research, but it is written in a style of high literary excellence." He concluded: "No one can read the historical record of the 2nd Battalion... without being grateful to Major Mainwaring for the happy manner of its preparation."

In 1912 Mainwaring edited a new edition of Sergeant-Major C.V. Brumby's recruits' guide *A Pocket History of the Royal Dublin Fusiliers.* Finally, his oddly titled final book, *Fishing and Philandering,* would not be published until September 1914.

Crucially, Mainwaring was subject to bouts of debilitating illness. During manoeuvres in September 1913 he suffered so severely from colitis that he was forced to return to Gravesend ahead of his battalion. Haldane was of the opinion that, if the time came, Mainwaring should not be passed fit for overseas service.

By mid-1914 Haldane felt confident that "as far as could be judged from training in peace-time... my brigade would give a good account of itself in the field."[22] As to Elkington and Mainwaring, he considered that "they had both done good service in peace-time."[23]

2
Mobilisation

At a midday meeting on Wednesday 29th July, 1914, the British Cabinet decided that the European Crisis had become sufficiently threatening to warrant declaring a "Precautionary Period", as laid down in the newly revised Government *War Book*.

This decision was immediately communicated to the Chief of the Imperial General Staff (CIGS), General Sir Charles Douglas, in a letter from the Prime Minister, Herbert Asquith, who also occupied the post of Secretary of State for War. The Army Council accordingly opened their departmental *War Book* and at approximately 2pm dispatched cypher telegram No. 1 from the list of *Messages from the Army Council notifying preparation for war:* "Adopt precautionary measures detailed in defence scheme."

These "Priority A" telegrams were sent to the General Officer Commanding-in-Chief of each Army Command, the officer commanding each District and to each Coast Defence Commander. They in their turn communicated with the commanders of the units, formations, depots and stations under their command.

At about 5pm on 29th July the precautionary measures telegram reached General Snow at Shorncliffe, where he was completing schemes for the imminent annual training manoeuvres: "Coast defences were manned and garrisons sent to vulnerable points. For the 4th Division this meant manning the Dover, Sheerness and Harwich defences by Regulars until the Territorials could relieve them, and many other duties of a similar nature."[1] Each of the three battalions of the 10th Brigade stationed at Shorncliffe provided a detachment to form a composite battalion to defend the Isle of Sheppey until the Territorials were ready. The adjutant for this temporary unit was a 27-year old Lieutenant of the 1/R. Warwickshire, Bernard L. Montgomery. He wrote to his mother on 30th July: "We have a great many posts out on the shore round about & have to be constantly on the lookout. I don't know how long we shall be here. I don't think the whole army is mobilising although certain brigades certainly are. I think it is just a precautionary move so as to be not caught napping. They are very frightened of a hostile landing here, as the coast is very suitable for it all round here."[2]

In fact, other than the precautionary measures such as those being carried out by the future Field-Marshal along the southern shore of the mouth of the Thames, no mobilization had been ordered. Indeed, the British Government's unwillingness to be drawn into a European war was reflected in its indecisive approach to the question of mobilizing the army. The annual Territorial Force training was just getting underway and the Cabinet took the view that cancellation would be seen on the continent as tantamount to mobilization. They delayed their decision until Sunday 2nd August when the Territorial training and Regular Army manoeuvres were cancelled at 2.50pm and 6pm respectively.

In order to carry out mobilization both Territorial and Regular units had to return to their Peace Stations and, as we have seen, certain Territorial units were assigned to guard duties, especially on the railway lines to the BEF's embarkation ports. All this movement required numerous extra trains at a time of high civilian Bank Holiday rail traffic and it had to be completed before the mobilization railway time-tables could be implemented. The Cabinet's decision had therefore effectively made Wednesday 5th August the first possible day of mobilization.

The attempts of British diplomacy to forestall a major continental conflict were thwarted by the news, received in London late on 2nd August, that Germany was demanding unhindered passage for its army across neutral Belgium. Consequently, during the early hours of 3rd August (Bank Holiday Monday) Asquith, solely on his own authority, wrote out the following order for the CIGS:

> The Cabinet approves of mobilization. Please put the necessary machinery, messages, in order: the proclamation to be made tomorrow.

This message was delivered to the War Office by Lord Haldane at about 11am that morning. At 1.09pm it reached the hands of the Director of Military Operations, Major-General Henry Wilson, "who was aghast to read that the Prime Minister's order was incomplete. It sanctioned mobilization in the name of the cabinet (though the cabinet had not yet given any authorization), but not, as all the expeditionary force plans required, embarkation."[3]

All War Office plans for co-operation with the French army in time of war had been Wilson's responsibility and in all those plans it had been assumed that mobilization would be followed by the immediate embarkation of the Expeditionary Force. Indeed, they had been looked upon as one seamless operation, with the first embarkation train movements tabled for the Second Day of mobilization.[4]

In fact, the CIGS, his fellow members of the Army Council and the staff of the Directorate of Mobilization (who had been making their final preparations since 27th July), had been aware for at least 24 hours that embarkation would not run concurrently with mobilization. Asquith had told the Army Council on 2nd August that the Government had no intention of dispatching the BEF "at present." Eventually, at 4pm on 4th August, the Privy Council signed all the necessary orders and proclamations and at 4.40pm the War Office dispatched the *en clair* telegraph message: MOBILIZE.

The message was received at the 4th Division headquarters at Woolwich at 6.26pm and at 6.37pm it was repeated to Shorncliffe where it reached the 1/R. Warwickshire at 7.05pm. However, aside from administrative details there was little that could be done until the following day, the official First Day of Mobilization.

During the night of the 4/5th August the first reservists responded to the appearance of the mobilization posters pasted up by the police and reported to their Regimental and Corps depots. On going into the Reserve each soldier was provided with an identity certificate, which he used to draw his quarterly reserve pay, so it was obviously in his own interest to keep it safe. The certificate also contained full instructions as to where he was to report on mobilization, a railway warrant for the journey from his home to his "place of joining" and a three-shilling money order for subsistence on the journey. These only became valid when a General Mobilization was ordered and, to avoid their misuse during peacetime, railway clerks were instructed to accept them only if a mobilization poster was actually displayed on the station.

The "place of joining" for the Royal Warwickshire reservists was the Regimental Depot in Warwick. Private R.G. Hill was among them:

"What a meeting of old friends! All were eager to take part in the great scrap which every pre-war soldier had expected. At the depot all was bustle, but no confusion."[5] Having passed a preliminary medical inspection they collected their "personal equipment, clothing and necessaries" and "In the mobilization stores, every reservists' arms and clothing were ticketed, and these were soon issued, with webbing equipment."[6]

Once they had changed into uniform and were fully equipped they made arrangements for the disposal, or collection, of their civilian clothes and prepared to move off in parties to their battalion. According to Lieutenant John Knight-Bruce, on the staff of the 3rd (Reserve) Battalion at the Warwickshire depot, the mobilization was a "great success; everything worked smoothly except that all the Reservists turned up on the first day instead of taking three days to come in, which had been expected." However, the battalion having only recently returned from India it "had less than the average number of serving soldiers fit to go out, but [it] got back a lot of men who had only recently passed to Reserve [so] it took out very few men who had only been three years with the Colours." Moreover, in this regiment "special attention had been paid to the fitting of the Reservists boots" when they came for their annual musketry course.[7]

The first Warwick reservists, a party of 83, reached Shorncliffe at 9.15pm on the First Day of Mobilization, together with Captain J.B. Haddon, 2nd-Lieutenant T.M. Bullock and 2nd-Lieutenant W.N. Boocock from the 3rd Battalion. On the following day, 6th August, the composite battalion returned from the Isle of Sheppey and at 7.15pm 288 reservists turned up from Warwick, as did Major W.C. Christie from an OTC appointment.

In his *Memoirs* Montgomery recalled his part in the Warwickshire's mobilization in the following terms:

> The mobilization scheme provided amongst other things, that all officers' swords were to go to the armourers' shop on the third day of mobilization to be sharpened. It was not clear to me why, since I had never used my sword except for saluting. But of course I obeyed the order and my sword was made sharp for war. The C.O. said that in war it was advisable to have short hair since it was then easier to keep it clean; he had all his hair removed with the clippers by the regimental barber and looked an amazing sight; personally I had mine cut decently by a barber in Folkestone. Being totally ignorant about war, I asked the C.O. if it was necessary to take any money with me; he said money was useless in war as everything was provided for you. I was somewhat uncertain about this and decided to take ten pounds with me in gold. Later I was to find this invaluable, and was glad I had not followed his advice about either hair or money.[8]

Meanwhile, in Whitehall, indecision reigned. On the afternoon of 5th August the Prime Minister had summoned a War Council and what the secretary, Captain (later Lord) Hankey, called a "notable company," Asquith described as a "rather motley gathering" and Henry Wilson dismissed as "an historic meeting of men, mostly entirely ignorant of their subject," attempted to decide on the destination and composition of the BEF.

The War Council soon discovered that as regards the general destination of the BEF they had little choice but to accept the existing War Office scheme since, as Hankey later wrote, their plan "for co-operation by our Expeditionary Force on the left of the French Army had been worked out by the two Staffs in great detail, and this could not be said of any other plan." Actually, there were no other plans, only vague schemes. Nevertheless, it was not until 12th August that, at a lengthy meeting, Wilson, Field-Marshal Sir John French (Commander-in-Chief designate), Lieut.-General Sir Archibald Murray (Chief of Staff designate), Colonel V.J.M. Huguet (French military attaché in London) and two other French officers, finally convinced Lord Kitchener, the Secretary of State for War, that the BEF should concentrate at Maubeuge, as always planned.[9]

So far as the composition of the BEF was concerned, Wilson had already told the French that the British would send five infantry divisions, taking as his authority a ruling given by Asquith on 6th May 1914 that he would "if necessary, sanction the dispatch of five, not four infantry divisions to Europe."[10] Prior to this ruling the requirements of home defence had apparently dictated that two infantry divisions should be retained in case of enemy landings. However, the editions of the BEF's secret *Disembarkation Tables* and *Instructions for Base Commandants* current at the outbreak of war (they were printed in March and July 1914 respectively) had been compiled on the assumption that all seven divisions (six infantry, one cavalry) would be transported to France to form the BEF and that the 4th Division would be the last of all to move, embarking on the 12th and 13th Days of Mobilization. The War Council meeting on 5th August recommended the dispatch of all six divisions, but following an indecisive meeting of the Cabinet, Kitchener announced that only four infantry divisions and the Cavalry division would be dispatched immediately and that a fifth infantry division would follow "when circumstances permitted;" there was no mention of a sixth division. The 4th and 6th Divisions were those held back.[11]

At Shorncliffe Haldane clearly knew, even before the outbreak of war, that the 4th Division "might be retained temporarily in the United Kingdom for purposes of home defence,"[12] so the contents of two telegrams that arrived for him during the 7th August cannot have come as a great surprise. The first "came stating that four divisions go first; presume that we shall follow which will give me more time for training."[13] The second arrived whilst Haldane was at dinner and ordered the 10th Brigade and a battery of field artillery to York for home defence duties.

The Brigade was railed north the following morning and initially it was divided between York (1/R. Warwickshire and 2/R. Dublin Fusiliers) and Darlington (2/Seaforth and 1/R. Irish Fusiliers). However, two half battalions (including that of the 1/R. Warwickshire containing Lieutenant B.L. Montgomery) went to Cromer more by accident than by design before rejoining the Brigade at York on 9th August.[14] The War Diary of the 2/Seaforth is the only one to remark on the disruption to mobilization by their commitment to home defence: "owing to the hurried move... before mobilization completed, everything left in considerable confusion at Shorncliffe, paylists, etc., not closed and baggage, etc. not stored away. Some transport horses and vehicles had to be left behind also."[15]

Suspect spies and invasion scares along the north-east coast notwithstanding, a good deal of time was spent by the brigade in hardening the reservists: "It was highly probable that as soon as they were landed in France they would find themselves called upon to march long distances, carrying, of course, the soldier's heavy equipment, and therefore every hour's preliminary tramping on the roads would tell in their favour when the hour of trial came. Route-marching at daily increasing distances was therefore carried out, and a perceptible improvement became noticeable. The reservists of the Seaforth Highlanders, however, who like men of all kilted battalions had shoes issued to them, but who when in civil life had habitually worn boots, soon developed sore heels, and for some weeks there were several who, with the best intentions, were unable to keep pace with the column...".[16]

For platoon commanders such as Montgomery route marches and manoeuvres meant that "every evening we inspect all the men's feet to see that they haven't got blisters, etc., & also to see that they wash them. If you left a man alone he would never wash his feet; it is rather a smelly job inspecting feet! But it is most important, as if your men can't march they are of no use."[17]

The Brigade moved south by rail to Harrow on 18th August and the Division was concentrated there by 20th August, having been relieved of its home defence role by Territorial and Yeomanry forces. At Harrow there were two more days of route marching, and according to reservist Pte. Hill of the Warwickshire: "By this time we had welded together, and were a really fine body of men, hard as nails, average age about twenty-five, and every man with the idea that he was equal to three Germans! Splendid men, enthusiastic, and brave, going to fight they thought, for a righteous cause."[18] Snow was "very thankful that we had had those few days to get feet and boots in order instead of being rushed overseas like the other four Divisions had been. It made all the difference to us later."[19]

The whole of the 4th Division was moved to Southampton in 73 trains provided by three separate railway companies from seven stations in the Harrow area between 10.25pm on 21st August and 2.20pm on the following day. A remarkable example of *ad hoc* planning that seems to have functioned without a hitch.

The headquarters of the 10th Brigade arrived at Southampton at about 3am on 22nd August and embarked aboard the SS *Caledonia*, along with the 1/R. Warwickshire and 2/R. Dublin Fusiliers, while the 2/Seaforth and 1/R. Irish Fusiliers embarked aboard the SS *Lake Michigan*. The two vessels left Southampton between 10.30am and 11.30am and arrived at Boulogne that evening. The *Caledonia* docked and disembarked some transport, but the troops stayed aboard, as they did on the *Lake Michigan*. The following morning, Sunday 23rd August, the *Caledonia*[20] disembarked her troops at about 5am and those aboard the *Lake Michigan* were disembarked by a little after midday.[21] The battalions formed up on the quayside and were marched away to rest camps on the northern outskirts of the port, near the Colonne de la Grand-Armée.[22] They remained there until the evening when they were marched out in four parties and at Boulogne boarded four "very long trains" between midnight and 4.03am on Monday 24th August, destination unknown.

3

The Battle of Mons

The movement to France of the four infantry divisions and single cavalry division that first made up the BEF was accomplished according to detailed instructions and complex interlocking railway and cross-channel shipping timetables that had been worked out in collaboration with the French general staff since 1910.

The rail movements from the ports of disembarkation to the areas of concentration were entirely controlled by the French and were practically completed by 20th August, when the BEF "was assembled in a pear-shaped area between Maubeuge and Le Cateau, about twenty-five miles long from north-east to south-west, and averaging ten miles wide. The cavalry was at the north-eastern end, ready to join hands with the French Fifth Army."[1]

On 21st August the BEF started to move forward on the left of Fifth Army in compliance with the wishes of General Joffre, the French Commander-in-Chief. By the morning of Sunday 23rd August it faced north and east, occupying, from left to right, the line of the canal from Condé to Mons, thence in a sharp salient north-east round Mons to Obourg and from there south and east to Grand Reng via a line that took in Estinne-au-Mont and Peissant; a total front of about 27 miles.

The extreme left at Condé was held by the 19th Brigade, recently formed from battalions of Lines of Communication troops and in touch on their left with the French 84th Territorial Division. Between the 19th Brigade and the eastern outskirts of Mons came II Corps, commanded by General Sir Horace Smith-Dorrien,[2] comprising the 5th Division on the left, lining the canal, and the 3rd Division on the right, holding the salient round Mons. The line south and east to Grand Reng, forming the right flank of the BEF, was held by I Corps, commanded by General Sir Douglas Haig. It comprised the 2nd Division (on the right of the 3rd Division) and the 1st Division to the right again, with the French Fifth Army to their right.

The independent 5th Cavalry Brigade was also posted on this flank, before being withdrawn, while the Cavalry Division was echeloned behind the 19th Brigade and the 5th Division on the left.

The main weight of the German assault fell on II Corps, opening in earnest before 9am on 23rd August at the eastern end of their line when German artillery fire opened on Obourg. By 10am the British infantry in the Mons-Obourg salient was heavily engaged and the attack was spreading slowly to the west along the line of the canal.

The course of the day's fighting at Mons has been recounted too many times to need detailed repetition. In brief, the steadily increasing German pressure along the entire II Corps line (about 15 miles long, including the 19th Brigade) and in particular the ferocious fighting in the Mons-Obourg salient began to tell. Smith-Dorrien had known from the outset that there would be "certain withdrawal from the untenable salient at Mons"[3] and had accordingly selected a main position some one to three miles to the south of the outpost canal line. Having fought the enemy to a standstill it was to this main position (about 12 miles long) that II Corps retired, without panic and as and when it seemed appropriate: "there was no uniformity of the movement from the outpost line... the characteristic obstinacy of the British infantry, which has always fought on without much regard to what was happening in other parts of the field, was thus early made manifest."[4] Even allowing for the British having destroyed a large number of bridges over the canal the enemy made little attempt to close up on the new position and the night passed relatively quietly. The troops of II Corps had borne the brunt of the fighting and had sustained by far the heaviest casualties of 1,600 all ranks, killed, wounded and missing. Nevertheless, they were in good heart, having aquitted themselves magnificently against an enemy overwhelmingly superior in numbers.

During the late afternoon and early evening it had become clear from RFC reconnaissance reports on German troop movements that enemy attacks would continue to develop on the following day and Sir John French sent the following message to Smith-Dorrien at 8.40pm:

> I will stand the attack on the ground now occupied by the troops. You will therefore strengthen your position by every possible means during the night.[5]

Meanwhile, disturbing news was arriving at the British GHQ regarding the state of the French Fifth Army. At about midnight this was confirmed when Sir John French received a message from General Lanrezac, its commander, to effect that his troops would commence retiring at 3am on 24th August. This would leave both British flanks entirely in the air and Sir John French was therefore left with no alternative other than to order a retirement.

Smith-Dorrien received this order at about 3am.[6] There being no signal communication between GHQ and II Corps, it had been carried by his senior staff officer, Br.-General G.T. Forestier-Walker. Smith-Dorrien learnt that II Corps was "to retire to the neighbourhood of Bavai in concert with the I Corps on its right. The retirement was to commence at 5am, and as regards the two Corps, co-ordination was to be arranged by the Corps Commanders in consultation."[7]

Daylight was already beginning to show along the rim of the horizon when Smith-Dorrien received the retirement order and sunrise was at 5am.[8] Smith-Dorrien at once advised Sir John French "that it would be well after daylight before any orders could be carried out... and that, before a retirement could commence, my impedimenta (closed up for battle) must be got away and the roads cleared." He concluded by saying "I have told you this so you may realise the situation and that the operation we are embarking on is one of the most difficult which can occur, namely, breaking off a fight at its hottest and adopting retirement tactics, without offering great advantages to an enemy."[9]

The retirement orders received by Haig at I Corps (by wire at 1.27am)[10] were both earlier and in more detail, in that they instructed I Corps to cover the retirement of II Corps. However, I Corps was not as closely beset by the enemy as II Corps and by dint of motoring to the 1st and 2nd Division headquarters in person to issue orders, Haig managed to get his two divisions away at 4am and 4.45am respectively. By force of circumstance the roles were therefore reversed and II Corps covered the retirement of I Corps.

According to Forestier-Walker, Haig and Smith-Dorrien met at II Corps Headquarters at about 4.30am[11] and in Smith-Dorrien's words they "settled on a course of action."[12] A warning order had already been issued by Smith-Dorrien, but orders to clear the roads of transport did not reach the brigades of the 3rd Division (the first of II Corps to retire) before 4.30am[13] and "it was 6.30am before the 3rd Division... sent orders to its first brigade, the 8th, to fall back."[14]

The German artillery had opened a heavy bombardment of the II Corps front before dawn, starting at the eastern end and steadily extending westwards and "by 5.15am a general infantry attack was rapidly developing."[15] As the 3rd Division moved off, its rearguard fought vicious actions against waves of German infantry in and around the mining villages of Ciply and Frameries, the 2/South Lancashire (7th Brigade) losing between 200 and 300 men when they were caught by enfilade machine-gun fire. Nevertheless, the 3rd Division withdrew towards Genly in good order and comparatively unscathed, having inflicted "very heavy losses"[16] on an enemy who thereafter kept his distance.

The 5th Division's withdrawal was more costly. On its right flank three battalions of the 5th Brigade (detached from the 2nd Division the previous night to fill a gap between the 5th and 3rd Divisions) withdrew under orders from I Corps at 9am, leaving the 5th Division's flank insecure. On this right flank the 13th Brigade and two battalions of the 15th Brigade therefore began to withdraw at 10.30am, covered by the 14th Brigade. Sadly, the message did not reach the 2/Duke of Wellington's (13th Brigade) and a battery of the 27th Brigade, RFA, and the battalion lost around 400 men before they completed a fighting withdrawal and got the guns away. By 2pm the 13th and 14th Brigades were disengaged and preparing to march south-west towards Bavai.

On the 5th Division's left flank the 19th Brigade and Major-General Edmund Allenby's Cavalry Division had withdrawn far enough by 11.30am to uncover that flank to a rapidly developing German threat. Major-General Sir Charles Fergusson, commanding 5th Division, at once asked for help from Allenby who immediately sent back two cavalry brigades that, together with the 1/Norfolk and 1/Cheshire (15th Brigade), the 119th Battery, RFA, and later the 1st Cavalry Brigade, formed a rear-guard to the division. They held up the German advance in the area of Quiévrain, Audregnies and Elouges before breaking off and retiring: "They had held off from the main body of the 5th Division the pursuit of a whole German corps, but at heavy cost."[17] For example, the 1/Cheshire did not receive the order to retire and were cut off. They fought on as long as their ammunition lasted and it was not until 7pm that the few survivors surrendered.

That night the British line lay roughly west to east through Bavai from Jenlain to Feignies. During the day's withdrawal the 3rd Division had smoothly changed places with the 5th Division and the latter was now on the right of II Corps. Since the 3rd Division had been able to retire first it had marched south-westward, to the west of Bavai. The 5th Division then withdrew directly southwards and slotted in on the eastern flank of II Corps and was thereby relieved from "its difficult position upon the threatened western flank."[18] A remarkable achievement during the first stages of a fighting retreat.

The day had been one of glaring heat and the men were thirsty, hungry, and above all exhausted as they stumbled into their resting places that night, only to be greeted with the news that they would be marching south again in only a few hours. According to Smith-Dorrien, the men of II Corps were "tired, hungry, but extremely cheerful, and they all felt that they had done well, which no doubt they had."[19]

II Corps suffered 2,000 casualties on the 24th, bringing its total to 3,600 over the two days, an important loss of strength, but not crippling. I Corps had lost 100 casualties on the day to add to the 40 of the previous day, so as yet it had been hardly touched.

At 6pm Smith-Dorrien reported to Sir John French at advanced GHQ at Bavai. He descibed to French "the situation in the 2nd Corps, and asked for instructions as to further movements."[20] The Commander-in-Chief knew that the French on his right flank were already ten miles to the rear of the British positions and he had therefore decided to withdraw a further 15 or 20 miles to a position running through Le Cateau. He told Smith-Dorrien that I Corps was going to start at 5am:

> I remonstrated, saying that unless we moved early it would be a case of that day [24th] over again, when orders had been issued too late to avoid the enemy coming to close grips.[21]

It was therefore agreed that Smith-Dorrien would get his transport on its way by midnight and that all his troops would be south of the Jenlain-Bavai road by 5am.

However, the line of retreat was partially blocked by the Mormal Forest, a piece of mixed woodland about nine miles long and three to four miles wide, but without a road through it from north to south. To attempt to pass the whole force down the west side of the forest "would mean, practically, a flank march across the front of an enemy greatly superior in numbers and already threatening his western flank; to pass entirely to the east of it was impossible owing to the proximity of the French."[22] The Commander-in-Chief therefore decided to split his force and ordered I Corps down the east side and II Corps down the west side of the Forest.

Meanwhile, the French Cavalry Corps, commanded by General Sordet, was passing across the II Corps line of retreat from east to west and delayed Smith-Dorrien's "impedimenta" getting away as early as planned. Consequently, the main bodies of the 5th Division did not move off until 3am and those of the 3rd Division not until 5am. They had long, hot, fatiguing marches ahead of them.

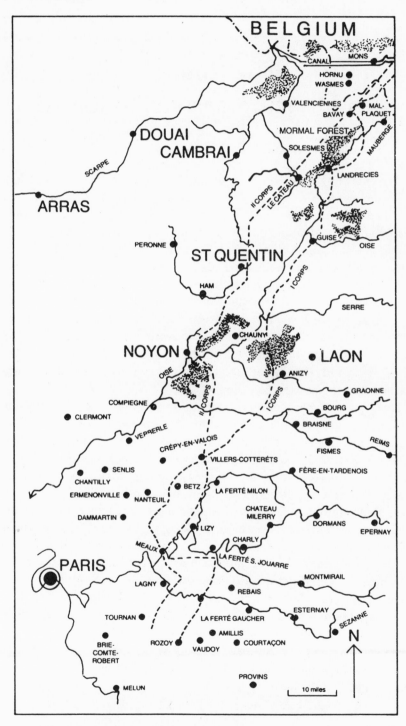

THE RETREAT FROM MONS 23rd AUG.–5th SEPT., 1914

4

The Retreat
4th Division arrives to join II Corps

General Snow and the Staff of the 4th Division had disembarked from the SS *Cestrian* at Havre at about midnight on 22nd August and made their first headquarters at the Hotel Continental. A divisional headquarters advance party, comprising Lieut.-Colonel A.A. Montgomery, Lieut.-Colonel F.P.S. Taylor and Captain H.J. Elles, left at 7am the following morning, reached Amiens at about 11.30am and then went on to Valenciennes where they saw Lieut.-Colonel G.D. Jebb, the Deputy-Assistant Quartermaster-General from GHQ. "But there were no orders to hand as regards detrainment of the Division. It was therefore decided that the party should return with the Lieut.-Colonel Jebb to Le Cateau to GHQ. Information was there received that the Division would detrain at and near Busigny. The advance party reached Busigny at 3am, 24th August."[1]

The main divisional headquarters party left Havre at 11pm on the 23rd, going first to Rouen and reaching Amiens early on the 24th. Here Snow interviewed the Inspector-General of Communications, Lieut.-General F.S. Robb, who (since he did not mention it) was apparently unaware that the BEF was falling back. Snow reached Busigny at 4pm on the 24th and found that Captain Elles had been to GHQ that morning and collected orders, the gist of which was that the divisional headquarters was to go to Busigny, the 10th Brigade would detrain at Le Cateau and then march to Beaumont. The 11th Brigade would also detrain at Le Cateau and then march to Troisville, and the 12th Brigade would detrain at Bertry and then march to Montigny and Ligny. The divisional artillery was to detrain at Busigny and Bohair, concentrate beside the Le Cateau-St. Quentin road at Premont and then move forward to more advanced positions.

Snow was swept off by car to GHQ at Le Cateau where he was briefed on the situation by his old friend Major-General Henry Wilson, the deputy chief of staff:

I also gathered that I was, as soon as I could collect enough troops, to push north and intervene between the enemy and the hard-pressed 3rd and 5th Divisions and cover their retreat even if my Division got decimated in doing so.[2]

I was also told that the idea was to fall back on the Le Cateau-Cambrai position and *there accept battle* and that the position was being prepared by impressed labour and that the position of my Division would be about Beauvoir and Cattincourt.[3]

Together with Br.-General W.H. Bowes (one of GHQ's liaison officers with the French) Snow went off to inspect the Le Cateau-Cambrai position and found it "fair", though there was no sign of prepared positions or impressed labour.[4]

The divisional headquarters was now transferred to Inchy and orders were issued from there for the moves on the following day, the 25th. The 10th Brigade was to move to St. Python to arrive there by 4.30am, the 11th Brigade was to move to Briastre by 4.30am, and the 12th Brigade was to move to Viesly by 4am. In the meantime the Second Line Transport was to go to Ligny and remain there under escort of the 2/R. Inniskilling Fusiliers (12th Brigade). Two squadrons of the North Irish Horse attached to the 4th Division were to be positioned at Solesmes. But the division's order of battle was far from complete, being without its "cyclists, heavy battery, engineers, the greater part of its signal company, train, ammunition column and field ambulances."[5] The divisional headquarters opened at Briastre Church at 4.30am on 25th August.

The 10th Brigade had started arriving at Le Cateau during the morning of 24th August, the headquarters, its signal section and the 1/R. Warwickshire first, followed by the 2/R. Dublin Fusiliers, and then in the afternoon the 2/Seaforth and 1/R. Irish Fusiliers. Private Hill remembered that "the town was in confusion ... refugees, troops, and ammunition columns creating a dust that choked us."[6] Each battalion in turn waited while its transport was unloaded, then formed up and marched away north-west along the road to Cambrai and thereby had their first experience of the notorious pavé road surface.

Captain Harold C. Hart of C Company, 1/R. Warwickshire, recalled it as "a stiff climb, uphill all the way, the day was very hot, without any shade from the poplars along the roadside, and the men found it very trying, but with every sympathy for them, many of whom were still, no doubt, rather soft, it was necessary to give stringent orders with regard to water and to prevent the men giving their water bottles to the willing and well-meaning small boys to take away to fill."[7] Moreover, as Private Hill recollected: "Civilians offered us foaming jugs of weak beer, but discipline was so strong that to accept it meant court martial."[8]

The battalions marched for about four miles before turning off in the area of Inchy and Beaumont and made their bivouacs, while Br.-General Haldane set up his headquarters in the Beaumont Brewery.

During the early evening Captain N.P. Clarke of the 2/R. Dublin Fusiliers was summoned to the brigade headquarters and told to reconnoitre the road north to a proposed artillery position near Solesmes, "so as to be able to guide the column by night, if required to do so." Clarke and a volunteer escort in the form of the battalion boxing champion cycled north, only to find that the approach to the suggested position was impracticable for guns. Attempting to return to the battalion they were twice halted in Solesmes by nervous French soldiers who had no idea that there were British troops in the area, let alone how they were dresssed and equipped. On the second occasion it transpired that their interrogator was the local commanding general who clearly did not wholly believe their story, even after detailed explanations had been given. In the end the general said: "Although I am sure you are what you say you are, still these are unusual times, and perhaps you would not mind undressing, or giving me some proof that you are English." An amused Clarke declined to disrobe in order to prove his nationality and instead showed the general his identity disc "and explained to him the interpretation of the various hieroglyphics on it. He was then quite satisfied."[9]

On returning to his battalion at about midnight Clarke discovered that they were due to move forward to St. Python in less than two hours, and unsuccessfully attempted to snatch some sleep. His commanding officer, Lieut.-Colonel Mainwaring, was also awake:

> I did not get any sleep whatever, as I had to see that everything and everybody was ready to move.
>
> Later on orders to march northward arrived, and I was again busily employed supervising matters, and in arranging for the withdrawal of our company on outpost duty.[10]

This set a pattern of sleeplessness that would extend throughout the following nights. Whether or not Lieut.-Colonel Elkington of the 1/R. Warwickshire managed to get some sleep that night is not known.

At 2am on the 25th the brigade marched off north through Viesly to St. Python, on the right bank of the River Selle, where they halted and had some breakfast, usually just consisting of some tea: "Suddenly we heard the dull reverberating boom of artillery. We had got to the front at last!"[11]

The firing appeared to come from the direction of Valenciennes and Haldane told Lieutenant C.W.C. Wasey[12] of the 1/R. Warwickshire "to take a couple of cyclists and push forward towards Valenciennes ... and bring back such news as he could get of the situation."[13] The results of this reconnaissance are unclear, but Lieut.-Colonel A.A. Montgomery from divisional headquarters also scouted towards Valenciennes and reached Famars on its southern outskirts without meeting any of the enemy. Moreover, while "there were a great number of French Territorials on the Valenciennes road" he does not appear to have met any of the retiring 3rd Division or 19th Brigade either.[14]

Haldane attended a conference at 4th Division headquarters where he received "some not very definite orders." On returning to his own headquarters he issued orders at about 8am to withdraw the brigade to a position about Fontaine-au-Tertre Farm and its road junctions. Here the battalions dug in in the beet- and corn-fields, and in the orchards to the north, and awaited developments.

At about midday the 1/R Warwickshire were issued with not only their rations for the day, but also their emergency rations. Captain Hart considered this "an event to be remembered, as it was the last rations many received until the night of [the] 28th."[15] Hart went on to recall that:

> during the early part of the afternoon not only was the sound of guns close, but the burst of shells could be seen not many miles away on our left front, and as the afternoon wore on, the tide of battle could be seen, slowly but surely creeping towards us.[16]

At about 5pm some five or six enemy shells fired from two guns in the direction of St. Aubert dropped in and around the farmyard at Fontaine-au-Tertre. The 2/Seaforth lost one killed and four wounded as a result. Lieutenant B.L. Montgomery jotted down in his diary: "My first experience of shrapnel. It was not nice as we could not reply."[17]

Some French troops had withdrawn through the position at about midday, commandeering a wagon for their wounded as they went, but there had been little sign of the retreating II Corps. Haldane did meet some men of the 1st Battalion of his old regiment, The Gordon

Highlanders (8th Brigade, 3rd Division), "looking exceedingly tired." They told him "the names of some of the officers who had fallen, and from their account it was evident that the forces in front of us were considerably more numberous [sic] than our own."[18] Some British cavalry came through the position at about 7pm and some contact was made with the 19th Brigade as they marched south-east from Haussy to Le Cateau across the 10th Brigade's front. The bulk of the 3rd Division passed through the 11th Brigade around Briastre on the right of the 10th Brigade. At about 5pm the fierce heat of the day was broken by a drenching thunderstorm that continued as a steady downpour till about 7pm and under the lowering clouds the light faded early.

A little before dark Haldane sent for Lieut.-Colonel Mainwaring (and presumably his other battalion commanders as well) and explained "that the Brigade had to remain where it was until the whole of our troops in front had passed through."[19] These instructions were almost certainly given as a result of the receipt of the 4th Division Operation Order No. 1, issued at 5pm, that detailed the division's part in the further withdrawal of I and II Corps to the Le Cateau position, a line that would run from Seranvillers (later changed to Wambaix) in the west, through Caudry and Le Cateau to Avesnes in the east. The order made it clear that, while all unwanted transport could be sent back at once, the troops were not to move until further orders were received, i.e. after the final elements of the 3rd Division and 19th Brigade had marched in. The 4th Division was then to withdraw, with the 12th Brigade holding the line from Wambaix to Cattenières station (between Wambaix and Fontaine-au-Pire), and the 11th Brigade from there to Fontaine-au-Pire where they joined up with the 3rd Division. The 10th Brigade was to be in reserve about the divisional headquarters at Haucourt.

According to Captain Clarke of the Dublins it was their advance companies in the orchard to the north of the of the Fontaine-au-Tertre farmhouse that first made contact with the advancing enemy cavalry at about 8pm:

> Everyone was on the *qui vive*, and absolute silence was kept. Not until the advancing horsemen got within 20 yards of the line of trenches did the challenge ring out - 'Halt! hands up.' There was no reply, so the French language was tried - 'Halte, qui vive?' The column halted and appeared undecided, but there was no reply, and the column were seen to be edging away.

At once the order to fire was given to our men, and a burst of musketry broke out. The enemy ... broke and galloped off whilst we collected their casualties. Again an advance was made against another battalion, and again a rattle of musketry brought their forward movement to a halt and sent the survivors scurrying away. After this we were left alone, and the wounded Germans in front of our lines were brought in and attended to.[20]

Captain Hart recalled that they could hear the horses galloping away down the road and the eerie way that "for quite a long time their clatter could be heard until it died away in the distance."[21] In the Brigade War Diary the enemy cavalry are described as "Uhlans," a term used indiscriminately by the British to describe all German mounted troops. However, they were also identified as belonging to the "11th Regiment" and it therefore seems likely that they were patrols of the *11th Hussar Regiment (14. Kav. Brig., 9. Kav. Div.).*

It was now clear that most of the 3rd Division was in and orders were issued for the withdrawal of the 4th Division in accordance with the divisional Operation Order No. 1. The 12th Brigade moved off at 9pm and the 11th Brigade at 10pm. The battalions of the 10th Brigade started to move off quietly between 11pm and midnight.

In fact, by this time Sir John French had decided not to stand on the Le Cateau position after all. Reconnaissance reports indicating the great strength of the enemy to his front and news that the French to his right were falling back even further apparently left him, once again, with no other choice but to order a continuation of the retreat on St. Quentin and Noyon. This decision had been reached by 3.45pm, at which time Henry Wilson sent Smith-Dorrien a private note of the Commander-in-Chief's intentions. These were formalised in the BEF Operation Order No. 8 and issued at 7.30pm.

For the 4th Division this order meant that, having completed a withdrawal of nine to ten miles to the Wambaix-Fontaine-au-Pire line during the night, they would then have to set off again at 7am for the Le Catelet-Beaurevoir line.

However, daunting as the prospect seemed for the tired troops of the 4th Division, in comparision with the exhausted men of II Corps, they were almost as fresh as paint.

5
Le Cateau and the Retreat

For II Corps 25th August had been a hard, hot, physically demanding day, though thankfully there were only limited contacts with the enemy.

The 5th Division rearguard had two brief engagements before it reached the Bavai-Le Cateau road, but as soon as it did, at about 6.30am, "it was no further troubled; the Germans followed it up at no great distance, but never pressed the pursuit"[1] as it moved down the sunblasted, dusty road towards Le Cateau. The bulk of the Mormal Forest on their left kept off even the hint of a cooling breeze and the temperature soared. The main body of the division came in to the Le Cateau position between 3 and 5pm and the rearguard between 5.30 and 6.30pm, all soaked through by the thunderstorm. The division took up a position between Troisvilles and Le Cateau.

The rearguard of the 3rd Division saw little of the enemy as it moved down to Le Quesnoy, covered out to the west by the 19th Brigade and the Cavalry Division screen that was in touch with the French 84th Territorial Division as it withdrew from Valenciennes. Most of the British troops on this left flank funnelled south towards Solesmes, where British transport filled streets that were aleady clogged with slow moving queues of refugees fleeing from the advancing enemy. Eventually, between 6 and 7pm, the rain-soaked main body of the 3rd Division (8th and 9th Brigades) got through Solesmes and, as we have seen, passed through the 4th Division to the right of the 10th Brigade. They then crossed the Cambrai-Le Cateau road and moved into position between Audencourt and Troisvilles. The 7th Brigade, the 3rd Division's rearguard, remained covering Solesmes, with two battalions to the north of the town until after dark, when they too were withdrawn.

Sir John French's Operation Order No. 8 was issued from his headquarters at St. Quentin at 7.30pm on the 25th and gave instructions for the continued retirement. General Smith-Dorrien received this order at 9pm and issued his own orders for the renewal of the retreat to II Corps (now including the 19th Brigade) at 10.15pm. These ordered that "all impedimenta" was to move off at 4am, followed by the main bodies of troops at 7am.

However, by the time these orders were being issued the situation that they had been framed to meet had passed. Sir John French's order had instructed Allenby's Cavalry Division (with the 5th Cavalry Brigade attached) to cover the retreat on the north and west, but the 4th Division was withdrawing from precisely the ground that the cavalry would have to occupy to fulfil its orders. Moreover, Allenby did not receive his orders until after 11pm, at which time he had only the 4th Cavalry Brigade under his immediate control, much too small a force to retake the ground.

Allenby hastened to Smith-Dorrien's headquarters at Bertry, reaching them at about 2am. He explained his situation to the Corps commander and added that unless II Corps and 4th Division could resume their retreat *before daylight* it was his opinion that they would be caught and brought to battle by the Germans. Allenby also stated that "his division was too much scattered and exhausted to be able to give useful assistance in covering the retreat next day."[2]

Smith-Dorrien immediately summoned Major-General Hubert Hamilton, the commander of the 3rd Division, whose headquarters were close by, and asked him if he could get his troops on the move before daylight. Hamilton said that he still had units coming in and that he would be unable to get his troops ready to resume the retreat before 9am. After a short conference with Allenby, Hamilton, Forestier-Walker, Colonel J. Vaughan (GS01 Cavalry Division), Major R.L. Macalpine-Leny (DAAG Cavalry Division) and Lieut.-Colonel F.B. Maurice (GS02 3rd Division), and having gained Allenby's agreement to act under his orders, Smith-Dorrien concluded that:

> with the enemy in force close to our billets the only hope of withdrawing successfully was to strike a blow first and to retire under the confusion caused by that blow.[3]

The decision having been made, Smith-Dorrien advised GHQ that, since he was unable to withdraw safely, he was about to attempt to administer a "stopping blow" against the enemy. Orders were issued "for a delaying action, including full instructions for retirement, the latter only to be acted on when I gave the order."[4] Smith-Dorrien went in person to the headquarters of the 5th Division to inform its commander, Major-General Sir Charles Fergusson, of the decision to stand. The II Corps GS03, Captain Basil Walcot, RE,[5] was dispatched to General Snow's headquartes at Haucourt with a request that the 4th

Division protect the II Corps left flank. Two messages were also sent to General Sordet, one personal and direct, the other more formal and via GHQ, both asking that the French Cavalry Corps provide co-operation and support on this flank.

As regards Haig's I Corps, there was now no direct contact between them and II Corps, with the only signal communication being via GHQ. Therefore, when the 4th (Guards) Brigade of I Corps was attacked at Landrecies during the evening and night of the 25th and the seriousness of this skirmish was exaggerated by I Corps to the degree that they were prompted to ask II Corps for help, it was from GHQ that Smith-Dorrien received a signal asking him to send assistance to I Corps. His reply was "much regret my troops are quite unable to move tonight."[6] Later, in response to Smith-Dorrien's message informing GHQ of his intention to stand and fight, Sir John French told him that the "News from I Corps reassuring."[7] This intelligence may have eased Smith-Dorrien's mind, but by then he was immersed in fighting one of the most difficult of all battles: to deliver a "stopping blow" that would halt the enemy for long enough to disengage II Corps safely. To achieve this he had to rely on the 4th Division holding his left flank.

The first elements of the 4th Division, a half battalion of the 12th Brigade, began to reach the extreme eastern end of the division's appointed line between just south of Wambaix and Fontaine-au-Pire at about 1am. The rest of the brigade was in place from Esnes, eastward along the high ground north of the valley of the River Warnelle, to just beyond Longsart, by 5am.

The 11th Brigade began to reach its destination at Fontaine-au-Pire at 2.15am. A wrong turning was taken in the dark and when it was halted the column was strung out from Beauvois through Fontaine-au-Pire and then half way along a muddy field track toward Cattenières. As dawn broke, German cavalry and artillery could be seen pushing south on Cattenières and the brigade came under fire whilst being extricated and taking up its position to the right of the 12th Brigade, facing Fontaine-au-Pire with the Warnelle valley at its back.

As we have seen, the 10th Brigade had been the last to leave the position covering Solesmes and they too had a hard and trying march over roads wet and muddy after the heavy rain, to reach their reserve position at Haucourt.

Led by its transport the brigade marched first to Viesly. Captain Hart recalled that when they had passed through the village early that morning they "had been greeted by the inhabitants, but now it seemed utterly deserted except for a single dog whose incessant howls were the only signs of life in the place."[8] Because the division's field ambulances had not arrived the 2/Seaforth were forced to leave their dead and wounded in a cottage near Viesly.

Hart did not know the exact route that they followed:

> but it seemed as if we were continually winding along to our right (westward); and in the earlier part of the night, where every we went or turned, we kept seeing a burning village ahead of us, and evey time we saw it again it looked closer than when we had last seen it. We got to hate the sight of it.[9]

General Snow described the night as:

> very dark and the whole sky to the northward was lit up by what we thought were burning villages. As a matter of fact they were probably only big fires lighted to dry the men's clothes by after the soaking rain.[10]

Haldane also recalled the "inky dark, though it is true that to our rear the lurid glare of burning farms and haystacks shed a fitful light upon the scene."[11]

Captain Clarke, 2/R. Dublin Fusiliers, noted that from Viesly their route lay through Bethencourt, westward along the road to Cambrai as far as Beauvois, then south through Fontaine-au-Pire to Ligny and finally west again to Haucourt. According to Clarke:

> It was a most trying march. Men had been on the move since 2am the previous day. There had been little time for rest or food, as they were always on the *qui vive*, entrenching, getting soaked by the rain, shelled in the farm, and attacked by night. Several of the reservists also had come from some quiet employment which did not tend to harden the feet, or keep them fit to carry the heavy marching order kit they had worn all that hot August day. So the conditions for a night march were hardly ideal. Men did their level best (they always do that), but they fell asleep as they marched, and dropped from sheer exhaustion.
>
> I know that I, at times, staggered across the road, trying to keep awake. I had had no sleep the night before, nor the night we landed, and was very weary.[12]

During the march to Haucourt, Haldane and his headquarters became separated from their troops. He had accompanied the last company of the 2/Seaforth to leave the Solesmes position and then ridden to the head of the column that was led by the brigade First Line Transport. On reaching Beauvois and Fontaine-au-Pire they found the tail of the

11th Brigade and with them General Snow, who ordered the 10th Brigade to move through the 11th Brigade to Ligny and then on to its appointed reserve position at Haucourt. The 10th's transport thereupon speeded up and, like the 11th Brigade, took a wrong turning, in fact the very one the 11th Brigade should have taken.

With Haldane leading the way, and apparently accompanied by Snow, the brigade transport reached a village at about 3.40am. Here they halted and Snow rode off in search of his headquarters. It was not until daylight that Haldane discovered that the village was Cattenières, well in front of the divisional outpost line, and that his infantry was missing. A cycle scout back-tracked their route, but found no trace of them. At about 5.15am came the sound of firing from the south-west, in the direction of Longsart, within the outpost line and *behind* Haldane and his transport. The horses were hooked in and the convoy moved off as quickly as possible towrds Haucourt. Haldane went on ahead and was not aware until later that the tail of the column was fired on just as it left Cattenières. Indeed, the leading elements of the German 2. *Kavallerie-Division* had been extremely close and:

> had they arrived a few minutes earlier it is difficult to see how we could, almost defenceless as we were, and with a narow railway bridge in our rear, have extricated ourselves from the very awkward situation in which we should have found ourselves.[13]

In search of his infantry Haldane rode up the ridge slightly to the east of Longsart, passed through the outposts of the 12th Infantry Brigade digging in in a beet field on the foward slope, over the crest, down the "short, sharpish reverse slope,"[14] across the dry bed of the Warnelle and up the ridge to Haucourt. The transport followed and reached the village at 6am.

Snow had safely reached his headquarters in the mairie at Haucourt sometime earlier and between 5 and 5.30am was attempting to get a few minutes sleep while his staff prepared to issue orders to continue the retirement, in accordance with GHQ's Operation Order No. 8 which had arrived at midnight. Haldane arrived not long after Captain Walcot, who was carrying Smith-Dorrien's announcement that II Corps was going to stand and fight and its concomitant request that the 4th Division cover his left flank. Snow was awakened and responded immediately to the request by telling Edmonds "to say yes."

> Orders were then issued for the position to be taken up and strongly entrenched. ... In most cases however these orders, owing to the entire

absence of communications, except mounted orderlies, did not reach their destination.[15]

Snow, anxious to see his front line positions before the battle started, "snatched a cup of tea and an egg and ran out into the courtyard,"[16] commandeered a car, press-ganged Haldane into accompanying him and tore off, as he thought, towards Cattenières. His driver overshot the junction and as he was turning the car they saw the road they intended to take "swept by an outburst of shrapnel and at the same time I saw shells bursting all along the position and a good many stragglers began coming back from the ridge."[17] In the words of Captain H.J. Elles, the infantry were already "at it hammer and tongs."[18]

6
Le Cateau:
Confusion Reigns

The four battalions of the 10th Brigade had made their way to Haucourt quite safely without their commander. Very few accounts agree as to their times of arrival, but they all seem to have reached the village between about 4.30 and 5.30am.

The Royal Irish Fusiliers and the Seaforth halted close to the Haucourt cemetery after "very tiring and wearisome"[1] marches in the rain over greasy roads. The 4th Division's battalions were not yet equipped with travelling kitchens and since the 10th Brigade's cooks' wagons were still on their way from Cattenières the battalions were unable to draw rations for breakfast. They fell out and either threw themselves down to sleep among the stooks in a cornfield, or went to draw water from a farm nearby.

Marching westward on the road from Ligny to Haucourt the Warwickshire passed the First Line Transport of the 11th Brigade parked at the roadside and just before reaching Haucourt they turned south off the road "into a field in which were standing stooks of corn. ... Here we formed up in Mass, piled arms, and took off equipment, lay down and slept the sleep of weary and exhausted men."[2]

Immediately in front of them was the Haucourt-Ligny road, along which they had been marching, and beyond that the valley of the Warnelle, the dry bed of which was about 300 yards below them. On the northern side of the valley, about three-quarters of a mile away, was a long crest line about 100 feet above their position and topped by a hedge. Behind them the ground sloped up for about a mile. On their right flank a bridle-path from Cattenières to Caullery crossed the Haucourt-Ligny road at right angles and at the crossroads were two cottages and a few trees. The bridle-path crossed the Warnelle valley and went up the facing slope alongside a small quarry and was joined by various tracks and paths. To the north they could not see beyond the hedge on the crest line, to the west their view was blocked by Haucourt, to the east it was obscured by Ligny and the high ground round about, and to the south by more high ground.

Captain Hart described the nature of the loam covered chalk downland as

> fields of corn in stooks, crops of beetroot or open grass land with a few
> small hedges. There were undulations and ditches, cuttings or
> embankments along the roads and tracks which gave a certain amount
> of cover.[3]

The Dublin Fusiliers, "very wet and fairly tired,"[4] arrived to the right of
the Warwickshire, the Cattenières-Caullery bridle-path marking the
junction between the two battalions.[5] Lieut.-Colonel Mainwaring sent
his adjutant, Captain R.M. Watson, to seek for orders: "He returned to
say that there was no sign of the Brigade Staff, but that he had seen
Colonel Edmonds, of the Divisional Staff, who said we were to march
again at 7am, another 12 miles. I went to Colonel Edmonds myself, and
he confirmed the order, adding that the men were to consume their
iron ration, and asking me if the men could do it. I replied that they
could, after a couple of hours' rest and some tea."[6] So, under the
impression that they were to continue the retreat, they were moved off
the road "and the battalion were told to lie down and sleep for a bit.
The horses were sent away to water, sentries were posted and we lay
down."[7]

At about 6am the 2. *Kavallerie-Division* of Generalmajor Frhr. von
Krane, with the 4 and 7 Jager battalions attached, started to push
south-east from Wambaix and Cattenières towards the 4th Division
line. Some shells started to fall on both sides of the Warnelle, but
mostly on the northern side. This was the shell fire seen by General
Snow.

The 1/King's Own had been the last battalion of the 12th Brigade to
arrive and it was assembled in close formation on the brigade's right
flank north of the Warnelle when it was caught by the most
devastating, concentrated machine-gun fire from a range of about 800
yards. Their commanding officer, Lieut.-Colonel A. McN. Dykes was
killed and they sustained some 400 other casualties, killed, wounded
and missing by the end of the action. The regimental transport was
badly shot up and the terrified horses stampeded away, bringing down
the brigadier and the brigade major in their flight. From the southern
side of the valley Captain Hart looked up: "... a terrible sight was to be
seen; down the Cattenières road, near the quarry, poured the remnants
of ... 1st King's Own, while two of their wagons, the horses dead, lay on
the side of the road just above the quarry."[8]

The survivors were rallied "and all men who could safely use their

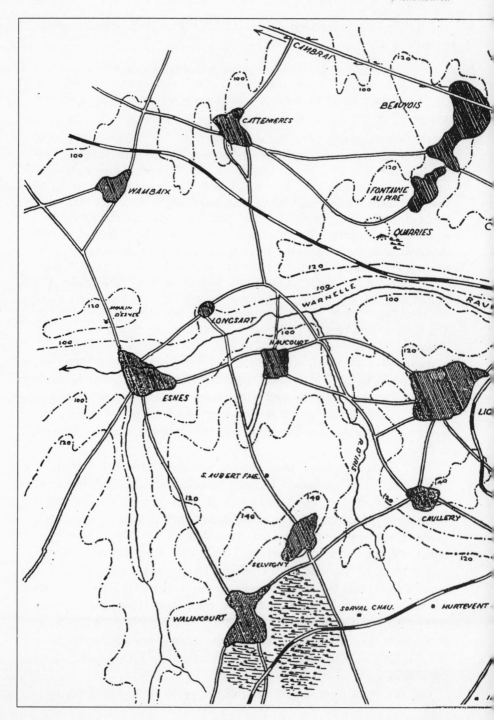

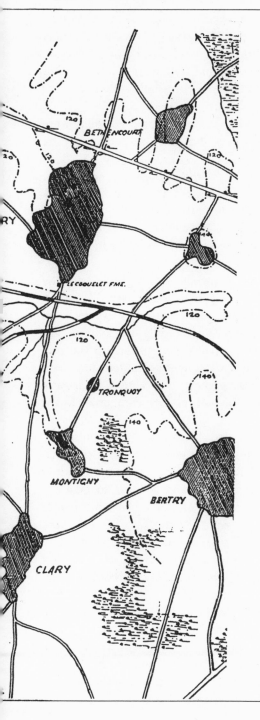

MAP ILLUSTRATING
THE ACTION AT
HARCOURT-LIGNY

BATTLE OF LE CATEAU
26 August 1914

(based on a sketch by
Major A.F. Becke
in his book
The Royal Artillery at Le Cateau
[RA Inst., Woolwich, 1919])

N
†

Scale 30mm/1 mile

rifles opened fire... upon the German machine guns, with immediate effect" in suppressing their fire.[9] Just as they were achieving this effect two or three batteries of German horse artillery[10] swung into the open between Wambaix and Cattenières, unlimbered, came smartly into action and plastered the King's Own with devastating shell fire for about 20 minutes.

In the midst of this the Warwickshire and Dublin Fusiliers were sorting themselves out and in the case of the Dublins adjusting to the realisation they they were not going to be retiring as they had been ordered. The Warwickshire hastily seized their rifles and equipment and "the companies were moved out of their massed formation."[11] A and B Companies moved forward and took up what cover they could along the sides of the Haucourt-Ligny road, while C Company moved behind one of the houses and the trees at the cross roads and D Company moved back.

Elkington decided to mount an immediate attack to relieve the pressure on the King's Own.[12] According to Montgomery: "The C.O. galloped up to us forward companies and shouted to us to attack the enemy on the forward hill at once. This was the only order; there was no reconnaissance, no plan, no covering fire. We rushed up the hill, came under fire, my Company Commander was wounded and there were many casualties."[13] In fact, Montgomery was with C Company and therefore was not with either of the two forward companies in the first wave.

As the first wave of the attack, led by Major W.C. Christie,[14] swarmed up the hill, Captain Hart (serving with C Company, commanded by Major D.A.L. Day) found Elkington on the road: "I was informed that he was attacking the ridge ... and ordered to take my men forward. The leading companies had got well up the hill before those in rear had got more than two thirds of the way up and were already being driven back under artillery, machine-gun and rifle fire."[15] The Warwickshire withdrew in reasonably good order and brought with them a company of the King's Own. Montgomery reckoned that they had finally retired from the ridge at about 8.30am and that the German fire had ceased by about 10.30am. In company with another officer he then went back onto the ridge and "fetched in Major Day who was lying with a broken leg."[16] In a letter home he described the attack as "terrible work as we had to advance through a hail of bullets from rifles & machine-guns & through a perfect storm of shrapnel fire. Our men behaved very well, though they were knocked down like ninepins."[17] He estimated in his letter that 200 men were killed or wounded, but the War Diary states that the battalion lost about 40 men killed, wounded and missing. They also lost three company commanders: Day (wounded), Captain P.E. Besant (wounded and captured) and Lieutenant C.F. Maunsell (wounded and captured).

When the Warwickshire withdrew they hastily dug in along the Haucourt-Ligny road with their left flank on the eastern edge of Haucourt and their right flank about 100 yards beyond the bridle-path crossroads where they were in touch with the Dublin Fusiliers. A second line was dug along the ridge about 200 yards to the rear.[18]

When the enemy first started firing the Dublin Fusiliers had been trying to get some sleep before continuing the retirement. Mainwaring recalled: "I fell in the battalion, and directed Captain Clarke to extend his company along the road, facing the firing, and Captain Higginson to do the same, slightly in echelon behind Captain Clarke, and left Major [H.M.] Shewan in charge of these two companies."[19]

These were A Company (Captain N.P. Clarke) and D Company (Captain G.S. Higginson),[20] with a platoon of B Company attached, and as they began to entrench so B and C moved back, but were seen to be going too far. Because the officers' mounts had been led away to be watered before the firing started Mainwaring could not get his horse for some time, but when he did he followed the two companies and "managed to stop the movement." He then took command of all the infantry he met "directing them to take up positions, and finally, getting hold of Captain Conlan's [B] and Captain Wheeler's [C] companies, placed them in position, and remained in a central place on the road myself."[21]

The "road" to which he refers was the Cattenières-Caullery bridle-path and his command post was at a point well over a mile behind his front line companies, with Caullery just behind him.

About 400 yards to his right front, between him and Ligny, were 27 and 134 batteries[22] of XXXII Brigade, RFA, supporting the 11th Infantry Brigade in their defence of Ligny. Mainwaring told his men that they could not "possibly retire as long as the two batteries remained in front"[23] of them and received two verbal messages from 4th Division staff that confirmed him in his decision to stand. The first was delivered by Captain H.I.R. Allfrey,[24] ADC to Major-General Snow: "'The General says he wishes you to hold on here to the end'. Then, turning in his saddle, he added: 'General Snow told me to say that this is a personal message from him to the regiment.'" Mainwaring replied "that the General might rely on us to do what he said." The second message was carried by Captain B.F. Burnett Hitchcock,[25] who said: "'It's only going to be a case of long bowls; no retirement.' Again I said there should be none."[26]

Neither the Dublin Fusiliers nor the Warwickshire received any orders from the 10th Brigade throughout the morning. This was not for the want of trying to reach them on the part of Haldane who, it will be remembered, had been accompanying Snow on a reconnaissance of the position when the enemy artillery had first opened fire. Haldane had immediately obtained Snow's permission to get back to his command, and on returning on foot to Haucourt had found the Irish Fusiliers and Seaforth and placed them just south of the village with a view to their covering the left flank of the Division and indeed the whole BEF.

But of the Warwickshire and the Dublin Fusiliers, Haldane found little sign. Several attempts were made to contact their commanding officers, but without success. It was known that the Warwickshire had attacked the ridge in support of the King's Own and thereby the 12th Brigade, but did not discover the whereabouts of Elkington until he was found by Captain T.H.C. Frankland, Haldane's Staff Captain, at about 3.30pm. Haldane had managed to communicate with Major Shewan, commanding the two companies of the Dublin Fusiliers to the east of Haucourt, but even he did not know the whereabouts of Mainwaring.

7
"...no-one left in front of us..."

There was a lull in the enemy shell fire from about mid-morning. It reminded Hart "of an Aldershot Field Day after both sides had expended all their blank" and it was at this time that stretcher bearers collected the wounded from the northern slopes of the Warnelle valley. There were also two visits from enemy aircraft "unmolested by anyone and easily observing our dispositions."[1]

At 2pm, shortly after their second aerial reconnaissance, the enemy opened a heavy bombardment along the high ground where Mainwaring and his two reserve companies of the Dublin Fusiliers were situated. This marked the start of an attack by Genlt. Graf von Schwerin's *7. Reserve Division (IV. Reservekorps)*, taking over the assault from the *2. Kavallerie-Division* who, according to one German observer, "had been thrown on the defensive and several regiments were cowering under cover behind the houses."[2]

Mainwaring considered that the "shrapnel fire that followed was, for some two and a half hours, by common consent, something altogether out of the common. Although shrapnel does little harm in comparison with its volume, the moral effect of lying still without being able to fire a shot in reply is very hard on even the strongest nerves."[3] According to Major A.R. Burrowes, second-in-command of the 1/R. Irish Fusiliers, by 4pm the enemy fire "had increased to a bombardment comparable with those so frequently developed later in the war."[4]

The situation in Mainwaring's reserve position was now becoming seriously fragmented. On the right flank C Company had been asked to provide cover for the two batteries of XXXII Brigade emplaced in front of them and had pushed out first a platoon under 2nd-Lieutenant J. MacN. Dickie and then a larger force under Captain W.H. Supple to about 300 yards in front of the batteries.

The guns of 27 Battery had been subjected to intense counter-battery fire to the point that it had proved impossible to replenish their ammunition through the bombardment. The crews had therefore been withdrawn to the shelter of a sunken road just behind the guns to await orders. At well after 5pm it was decided to run the guns out by hand, but it transpired that the gun trails "were so deeply embedded that they could not be lifted until the earth around them had been loosened."[5] Parties of volunteers moved back to the guns and under cover of the shields worked with picks to loosen the trails and in this way managed to haul out four guns and limbers and manhandled them to the sunken road. Under increasingly heavy shell fire two other guns had to be abandoned. "Forming up the four guns under cover they waited their time and then made a sudden dash to the south-westward, pursued by German shells - fortunately all were very short. These four guns saved."[6] They were got away across country, NCOs having been sent ahead to reconnoitre a route and cut the wire fences.

Mainwaring describes how at about "5pm one of the batteries [presumably 134 Battery] in front brought up their horses, and got their guns away at full gallop." He goes on to say that the "other battery [presumably 27] had suffered severely. We were told that two of its guns were out of action, and I could see that the men could not remain behind the shields."[7]

Captain R.M. Watson, Mainwaring's adjutant, remained with him throughout the bombardment and noted that the guns (again presumably 134 Battery) "began to go" at 4.45pm, but makes no mention of the infantry that Mainwaring claimed "had been slowly withdrawing for some time" and that by 5pm "had all passed away from the front and left front of our positions."[8]

Now that it was evident to Mainwaring "that there was no one left in front of us but the disabled battery"[9] he wrote a note to General Snow "explaining the situation, and asking for instructions" and Watson either "volunteered" or "was sent" - accounts vary - in search of the 4th Division headquarters. According to Watson he "met a Staff Officer who said that he knew nothing about us, but as all the guns had gone, we should retire. I went back and told Colonel Mainwaring this and we retired."[10] In his account Mainwaring says that Watson returned after about 20 minutes and:

> told me that General Snow and the Divisional Staff had gone, that no one remained to give an order of any sort, and that we were left alone.
>
> On this information I decided to retire, and, passing the word to everyone within sight to get ready, we, at about 5.30pm retired through the village [Caullery].[11]

It is not clear whether or not this retirement took place before or after 27 Battery got its four guns away.

Those who were "within sight" would appear to have been just the battalion headquarters and some stragglers - probably around 80 of all ranks. No attempt appears to have been made to contact either Captain Conlan's B Company or Captain Wheeler's C Company, who were comparatively close at hand. On Captain Watson's own admission: "We had completely lost touch with the two companies in the firing line and I understood that the other Companies [B and C] in support had already gone."[12] They had not.

B Company had one platoon in the front line at Haucourt and would therefore have had a strength of about 170 men in its reserve position. There is no account of what happened to it, other than the fact that it withdrew before C Company and that Captain Conlan was wounded and captured on 27th August.

At C Company Captain Wheeler had also seen infantry retiring on his left flank for some time, confirming Mainwaring's observations. When the guns of, presumably, 134 Battery also retired he sent an orderly to see if the battalion headquarters and B Company, which was to his left rear, were still in place. The orderly reported that they had all gone. Wheeler thereupon ordered his company to retire, including the detachment under Captain Supple that had been in front of the guns, and led them south through Caullery.

Meanwhile, as the afternoon progressed, so the situation in the front line became more and more confused. The garrison had been depleted when A Company of the Warwickshire had been withdrawn to act as escorts to some guns (probably 127 Battery, XXIX Brigade, RFA) as they retired from their position south of Haucourt. Captain Hart describes how the remaining troops were "strung along the road for about 600 yards from the edge of Haucourt" and comprised "about 300 of the 1st Royal Warwickshire, about the same number of the Royal Dublin Fusiliers,[13] some 40 or so King's Own and a few of the Royal Irish Fusiliers, some 600-700 in all."[14] In fact, the "few" 1/R. Irish Fusiliers comprised its A Company (Major R.A. Gray) with a platoon of B Company (Lieutenant A.V.Olphert) attached, who were holding the eastern end of Haucourt. The detachment of King's Own was commanded by Major R.G. Parker.

At about 4pm, while Haldane was on his way to confer with the recently located Elkington, the Germans switched some of their guns from bombarding the reserve lines to the front line which they continued to shell for about an hour. At this point Captain Frankland,

Haldane's Staff Captain, gained leave to go to his battalion, the Dublin Fusiliers, in their reserve position, and having "found them getting on all right" he then walked south, towards Caullery.

According to the War Diary of the Warwickshire, Elkington and 60 men retired on Ligny at 6.30pm. No reason is recorded for the retirement of the Commanding Officer and his small group, nor is there any explanation of why a substantial proportion of his command was left behind.

As darkness fell Major A.J. Poole,[15] second in command of the Warwickshire and the "slack officer" castigated by Haldane at Shorncliffe, "went off to seek for orders, and after being away some little time returned and merely said he could not get any instructions."[16] Poole had in fact discovered that the whole of the 4th Division appeared to have withdrawn and that the mixed force along the Haucourt-Ligny road was quite alone. In Poole's words: "As I was the senior officer there I assumed command of the force and decided to withdraw and make for Selvigny, where I was informed Head Quarters [of the 4th Division] had been during the day."[17] But things were not to be quite as straightforward as that.

Firstly, the enemy had occupied at least part of Haucourt, which had been empty except for British wounded and medical staff,[18] and exchanged fire with the British left flank picquets. Secondly, it seemed very likely that Ligny had also fallen into German hands.

Lieutenant Wasey was again selected to carry out a reconnaissance. "Meanwhile we waited, with not a little anxiety, for the position was to say the least, a perilous one. The men were very good, not bothering one with questions, though they well knew something was wrong."[19]

Wasey's report was not at all encouraging as it "led to the conclusion that it was more than likely that the enemy's forces were already behind us...".[20] There was a hushed consultation between the senior officers of the various detachments "with the result that it was decided that our position was impossible and that we should get out of it as best we could."[21]

The only route that seemed practicable for avoiding the enemy who, even in the pitch dark, was presumed to be using the well mapped roads, was the Cattenières-Caullery bridle-path, described by Clarke as "a track going south... but so faintly marked on the map that it was hard to distinguish by the aid of an electric torch."[22]

In the almost impenetrable darkness the orders to assemble in silence on the bridle-path were passed along the front line in hoarse whispers. The Warwickshire took the lead, followed by the details of the King's Own and the Royal Irish Fusiliers, with the Dublin Fusiliers bringing up the rear. Major Poole considered the bridle-path unsuitable for wheeled transport, so the Warwickshire abandoned their machine-gun section's limbered wagon and ammunition cart and the section was ordered to carry its two guns and their ammunition.

Major Shewan, Dublin Fusiliers, on the other hand, decided to retain their machine-gun wagon to carry their wounded (at least one of their machine-guns had been destroyed during the afternoon bombardment). Unfortunately it had been left in or near Haucourt, now partly occupied by the Germans, and the machine-gun section was sent off to try and retrieve it:

> Minutes passed, however, and still not even the bark of a dog broke the silence. Then suddenly we heard the lumbering of the gun limber as it was driven towards us. It came bumping across the field, the horses stumbling over the turnips. Then we had to hunt for a place where the gun could get off the field on to the road. The latter was four or five feet lower than the field, and had a good-sized ditch as well. At last, however, it was got off, after being run up and down the line, and it crashed into the cobbles of the Chaussée, luckily without being broken up, where it was loaded up with wounded.[23]

It was then swung on to the bridle-path and made ready to advance, but when an officer went forward to the head of the column to report that they were ready to move, it was discovered that the Warwickshire had already pressed forward into the darkness.

Believing that the whole column was closed up behind him Major Poole had moved off down the bridle-path towards Caullery. "The pace was necessarily slow, the halts long and constant and the march seemed interminable. Tired out, most if not all, slept as they marched, and several suffered from illusions brought on by fatigue and lack of sleep. The flames from Ligny alone lighted up and intensified the darkness of the night. Once a shot was fired but by whom, friend or foe, no one knew."[24]

At about 2am on the 27th they reached a village that Poole thought was Selvigny and there they halted and "falling like logs were utterly indifferent to anything but sleep."[25] It was not until daylight that Poole discovered that they were actually in Caullery.

When it had been discovered that the Warwickshire had moved off without them, Major R.G. Parker decided to lead his party of King's

Own independently of the rest. "Following a country track, they slipped past one village, in which there were Germans, skirted round several others, and halted at a farm where the farmer showed them much kindness and gave them food."[26]

Major Shewan took command of the remainder of the part of the column that had been inadvertantly left behind. They also moved south along the bridle-path, but at some point a turning to the east was taken and at 2.30am on the 27th the party stumbled into Ligny. "The men were very wet, fatigued and hungry and when we halted to ascertain our position and direction they immediately dropped into the puddles in the road and slept."[27]

At first light they left their wounded in the church, which was already filled with casualties from the day before, obtained a little bread from the local inhabitants and the column, about 400 strong, moved off along the road to Clary, with A Company Royal Dublin Fusiliers (Captain N.P. Clarke) leading. They knew that the enemy advance guard had passed through the village the previous evening and "in unknown strength in unknown places, might be met with at any moment."[28]

8
St Quentin:
"Unconditional Surrender"

It will be recalled that having visited the reserve position of the Dublin Fusiliers at about 4pm on the 26th and found them "getting on all right," Captain Frankland, Haldane's Staff Captain, had then walked south to Caullery. Here he gathered together some 50 men, made up of the transport personnel and cooks of the 1/R. Irish Fusiliers and stragglers of several other regiments, formed them into an *ad hoc* company and set them to guarding the northern approaches to the village in expectation of an attack from Ligny.

According to Frankland it was at about 6pm that Mainwaring (who believed it was about 5.30pm), Captain Watson and their Dublin Fusiliers arrived at Caullery. Frankland helped to sort them out and, "my corporate Coy., whom I had left for a moment, having dispersed,"[1] he went with them to Elincourt. In Mainwaring's own words he was "nearly done," so Frankland lent him the horse he was riding and "saw no more of him."[2]

Frankland and Watson pushed on from Elincourt to Malincourt with 30 to 40 men. Meanwhile, according to Mainwaring: "Unfortunately, owing to woods, wire, farms, etc., the other files did not keep touch with me, and when I reached Malencieux [Malincourt] I had only 40 men of the Battalion with me."[3] Before the Frankland and Watson party reached Malincourt they were "collared ... as escort to guns. The men were mounted on wagons and limbers. I rode on an off wheeler."[4] Frankland got off at Aubencheul hoping to find 10th Brigade head-quarters, but found only the 2/Seaforth transport. They moved on to Le Catelet where Frankland found the rear of the 4th Division column and eventually the 10th Brigade HQ that joined the column at Roisel.

When Watson and his party reached Le Catelet aboard the artillery limbers they were relieved of their escort duties and joined up with Captain J. Burke (Quartermaster of the Dublin Fusiliers), Captain Wheeler and his party of C Company that had also been carried on artillery, a party of the 2/Seaforth and the 10th Brigade transport.

By some circuitous route Mainwaring and his 40 men reached

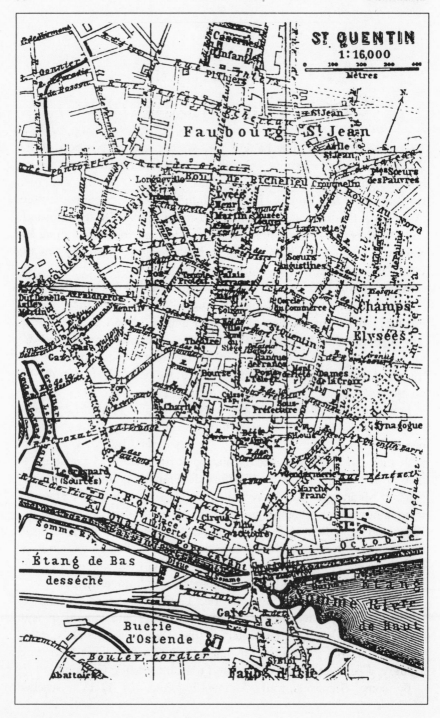

Malincourt "at dusk, and the men being thoroughly exhausted, I got them into a barn, told them they might consume their iron rations, and go to sleep."[5]

From this time until quite late on the following day, 27th August, Mainwaring's is the only first-hand account we have of the chain of events that befell him and his party and that led inexorably to the Mayor's office and the station courtyard at St. Quentin.

Mainwaring, after seeing that his men were settled:

> then went to try and find somebody to give an order or direction of some sort. I met Major Daniell,[6] Acting Brigade-Major of our Brigade. He expressed great joy at seeing me, asked how many men I had, attached 60 of the Warwicks, under a Special Reserve lieutenant,[7] to me, and promised to send me orders. I pointed out the house we were in to him, put a sentry on the gate, so that an orderly should find him, and spent most of my time there myself. I did not dare to lie down, as all the rest did, as I had nobody on whom I could possibly depend to wake me up. This was my third night without one wink of sleep of any kind.
>
> After some two hours or less I again went to see if I could find why no orders had reached me. I found a cavalry regiment just leaving, the last troops in the village, with the exception of ourselves. The cavalry colonel told me the retirement, his, at least, was on two villages, L'Empire [Lempire] and Rossay [Ronssoy], and left me. Consulting my map, I determined to march on the latter, as being the more southerly, and waking the men myself, started somewhere a little after midnight.
>
> Thursday, Aug. 27th, At 3a.m. we reached the village of Beaurevoir, which showed me we had missed the road in the night. I put the men into barns, but again stayed up myself. The strain was cruel, but I could trust no one else.
>
> At 5a.m. we marched towards Estree [Estrées], I determined to march on St. Quentin by Jongcourt [Joncourt] and Le Vergies [Levergies].[8]

Meanwhile, during the evening of 26th August, Smith-Dorrien had motored from his headquarters at Bertry to St. Quentin to report to Sir John French and organise trains to carry away his wounded and exhausted men. At St. Quentin Smith-Dorrien found the "Director of Railways, Colonel McInnes"[9] who said "the most he could provide was seven trains, and he was doubtful about that, and then only with the Q.M.G.'s consent."[10] Smith-Dorrien also discovered that the Commander-in-Chief had moved back 35 miles to Noyon, followed him there and arrived at about midnight on the 26th. He reported to Sir John, arranged with the QMG for as many trains as possible and immediately drove back and reached St. Quentin just as dawn was breaking.

Smith-Dorrien was accompanied on his return journey by a convoy of three or four cars carrying GHQ staff officers who were to assist in directing the footsore and exhausted officers and men of II Corps - mostly the 5th Division and the 19th Infantry Brigade - some more dead than alive and who were ready to drop in the streets of St. Quentin but had to be sorted into some semblance of order and kept going south towards Ham. Frederick Coleman, an American citizen, was one of the Royal Automobile Club's civilian volunteer owner-drivers attached to GHQ and he was in the convoy of staff cars that morning: "St. Quentin, on Thursday, August 27th, saw rare scenes and strange sights."[11]

Among the staff officers was Captain C.P. Deedes, a GS03 in the Operations Section at GHQ:

> The first thing we met was part of a Mechanical Supply Column, parked by the roadside and the officer sleeping peacefully in a house hard by: this seemed to indicate that things were quieter than we had supposed. We were soon undeceived! On arriving in the main street we met the head of the retreating Corps. Worn-out officers and men past caring for anything, worn-out in mind as well as body and hardly capable of taking in the simplest instructions, they trickled through the streets of St. Quentin. The infantry were often in parties of two or three men, mostly without packs and sometimes rifles as well; occasionally fifty or sixty men under an officer or two - the remnant of a battalion; occasionally a gun or two and half-a-dozen wagons - the remains of a brigade of artillery; then train wagons loaded with kits and wounded men, and so on.
>
> Our first job was to try to get the men into their right divisions - the sorting out into units must be done later. The first arrivals belonged to all three divisions of the Corps and were mixed up with stragglers from the cavalry and even from I Corps which was miles away to the east.[12]

Coleman and some of his fellow civilian drivers were also set to work sorting, marshalling and advising at the northern and north-eastern entrances to the town as the weary soldiery flowed slowly past:

> Jumbled together, inextricably mixed, each group convinced that their little remnant contained the only survivors of their individual command, confusion worse confounded was only to be expected.[13]
>
> Those who appeared to be positively unable to go on were stopped at the St. Quentin station to be sent by rail.
>
> Horse wagons full of wounded jostled the ambulances in the station

yard. Even the motor transport lorries, as they rolled past, paused to drop off their quota of maimed and bandaged men in khaki.

One young subaltern passed, sound asleep in his saddle and unmindful of all about him, his horse following the human current.[14]

*   *   *

Shortly after resolving to march on St. Quentin, Mainwaring and his party had met Lieut.-Colonel Elkington:

with about 100 of his regiment, the Warwicks, and joined forces, he, being the senior, taking over command. He told me he had already made up his mind to march on St. Quentin. I very much doubted our ability to get them as far as St. Quentin, but by dint of encouragement and pointing out that stragglers must become prisoners, and marching very slowly, and with many halts, we managed to reach that place between 12 mid-day and 1p.m.

Colonel Elkington sent me on to see what could be done, and I met General Smith-Dorrien in the town,[15] and told him the men were done. He told me it was a marvel that any of us had got away, that we had been up against four and a half to five German Corps, and that he would give us a train to Noyan [Noyon] if I could get one, and that if I could not he advised me to march some five miles further on the road to Ham, and join the 3rd Division. A member of his staff reminded him that it had marched from there, when he said: 'There are some details there; you had better try and join them.' I said I doubted if our men could do it, and that I would at all events try for a train first.

I sent this information to Colonel Elkington, asking him to march to the station, and proceeded there myself, only to find that all the railway staff had fled, and that there was no chance of a train. Colonel Elkington then arrived with the party, and we determined to try and make the men make an effort to get on towards Ham.

At this moment General Hobbs[16] arrived in a motor-car. He said that the Mayor would probably be able to get us a train, and certainly some food, so Colonel Elkington directed me to go and see him. I did so, taking an interpreter with me. The Mayor told me there was no chance whatever of a train, but that he would send us some food, which I asked him to expedite.

At this moment a breathless messenger handed a note to the Mayor, who, on reading it, became very excited, throwing up his hands, and exclaiming it was the end, all was lost. The room was full of excited Frenchmen, so I told my interpreter to tell me exactly what was in the note. He said that the town was surrounded, all exits blocked, that people in motor-cars were coming back, unable to get through, and that the Mayor was waiting to surrender the town. I was leaving the room when the Mayor caught sight of me and said 'Ah! your troops will spoil all. The Germans will shell the town now, and the women and children will be killed,' or words to that effect. I said 'You need not fear; if we cannot get our men away, we will not fight in the town. I must go and see my commanding officer." We neither of us doubted the authenticity of the Mayor's statement, for we had ourselves seen shells bursting only some seven or eight miles north of St. Quentin, more than three hours before.

Colonel Elkington agreed that we must not endanger the safety of the inhabitants by fighting in the town. I addressed my men, and he addressed his. I told mine that I would lead them out then and there, and try to get to Noyan [Noyon], a distance of 25 miles, if they would make the attempt, BUT NOT ONE MAN OFFERED TO COME. Colonel Elkington has also stated on oath that he made the same offer to his men with a similar result. The fact is the men could do no more for the time being. Their limit of endurance was reached. I considered it my duty to protect these men, who had so nobly done theirs. I still consider that it was so, and my conscience is quite clear. Their condition was admitted by the court, by mouth of the President.

He therefore directed me to sign a surrender, and while I was doing so he disarmed the men, putting their rifles and ammunition in one railway shed, and them in another.

As I rode back to the Mairie I saw terrified women dragging their children indoors, and everyone putting up their shutters. Everyone but ourselves and a few stragglers had fled, and as I rode up, my brain became obsessed with the one idea that our duty was to save nameless horrors overtaking these poor, defenceless creatures. It was Thursday afternoon; I had not slept since Monday morning; I had seen villages burning and others shelled. I could think of nothing else, and that is the whole truth, to which I have sworn on oath. The consequence was that when I came to sign the paper I felt my duty was to make our purpose quite clear. I wrote the names of the officers[17] and the strength of the party, and I said that as the men were unable to march away we would 'surrender unconditionally.' Even as I wrote the words I paused; but the state of my brain was such that I felt if I argued as to the conditions it might leave an opening for the Germans to shell the town and kill the civilian population, and I then felt my duty was to make no attempt at terms. Prostrated with mental and physical exhaustion, I wrote these words, convinced I was doing my duty and a noble act. This upheld me and was my one feeling throughout, and that, as to all else I have written here, I swear on oath.[18]

9
Major Tom Bridges' Timely Arrival

During the afternoon of 27th August elements of the 2nd Cavalry Brigade were ordered to provide a protective screen between St. Quentin and the advancing Germans. The force was commanded by Major G.T.M. Bridges[1] and comprised two squadrons, mostly made up of his own regiment, the 4th (Royal Irish) Dragoon Guards - a total of around 300 men - and two companies of French territorials. Bridges was ordered to hold off the Germans long enough to allow the final stragglers to get away and then to retire through St. Quentin at 6pm.

> The Frenchmen were dug in on a rise north of the town, a nice position, with a clear field of fire. I arranged with the commandant that he should stay there till 4p.m., but after visiting the outposts and returning about 2p.m. there was not a pair of red trousers in sight anywhere.[2]

J.H.O. Gibbs, a Chaplain attached to GHQ, passed through St. Quentin at about this time and found men "scattered about the town, propped up against the walls of houses, sleeping on pavements, or lying in gutters, numbed by fatigue and lack of sleep."[3]

Not long after this Captain Arthur Osburn, RAMC, the Medical Officer of the 4th Dragoon Guards, entered the Grande Place:

> The whole square was thronged with British infantrymen standing in groups or wandering about in an aimless fashion, most of them without either packs or rifles. Scores had gone to sleep sitting on the pavement, their backs against the fronts of the shops. Many exhausted lay at full length on the pavement. Some few, obviously intoxicated, wandered about firing in the air at real or imaginary German aeroplanes. The great majority were not only without their arms but had apparently either lost or thrown away their belts, water bottles and other equipment.[4]

Osburn estimated that there were several hundred men in the square, with more in the side streets, but he could see no officers.

Meanwhile, there had been a noticeable decrease in the flow of stragglers and "barring an occasional solitary lame duck, they seemed to have ceased coming down the Le Cateau road."[5] Lieutenant A.C.G. Harrison, Bridges' interpreter, rode into St. Quentin to check that the infantry had cleared the town, but on his return "reported the place swarming with stragglers, he could find no officers and the men were going into the houses and lying down to sleep."[6]

Bridges immediately dispatched Captain H.S. Sewell, 4th Dragoon Guards,[7] "with some hefty hench-men, farriers and the like" to get the soldiers out of the houses, to then assemble all the stragglers in the square, to commandeer bread, cheese and beer(!) "and to have it put down ready by portions on the pavement outside the Mairie, so that if we were pressed, as seemed quite possible, we should not have to waste time issuing rations."[8]

Mainwaring, having signed the "unconditional surrender," returned to the station:

> At about 4p.m. a cavalry subaltern [probably Lieutenant Harrison] rode into the station yard, calling the men to turn out and follow him. They utterly refused to. I explained the situation. He abused them and left. As time passed on it became evident that something had delayed the German advance, and I began to pray for darkness. I heard afterwards that the cavalry came from somewhere, and held them back.

> Later on a cavalry captain [probably Captain Sewell] arrived, accompanied by the same subaltern. He told me he could guide us out, when I at once said every man would thankfully come. By now I was in command as Colonel Elkington had left.[9]

Mainwaring's account is supported in part by Bridges, who explained:

> I conducted these negotiations through an intermediary, as I knew one of the colonels well and had met the other, and they were, of course, both senior to me.[10]

However, Bridges also said that having been told they were covered by a cavalry rear-guard and to hurry up and get out the men at the station held a meeting and then "refused to march on the gound that they had already surrendered and would only come away if a train was sent to take them." In response Bridges sent them an ultimatum "giving them half an hour's grace, during which time some carts would be provided for those who really could not walk, but letting them know that I would leave no British soldier alive in St. Quentin."[11]

Osburn's account is more colourful, recording that a mob of disorganised soldiery had assembled at the station and, so he had been told, they had "booed and cheered ironically" as a "Staff train" had steamed out. Moreover, he claims that Bridges had "harangued this disorganized [sic] mob" at the station with the result that one of the men had shouted back "'Our old man (his Colonel) has surrended to the Germans, and we'll stick to him. We don't want any bloody cavalry interfering! and he pointed his rifle at Bridges."[12] Unfortunately, Osburn, who "didn't much care what happened," became bored and wandered away, so the outcome of this supposed confrontation is unknown. It must be remembered that the Elkington/Mainwaring party had been disarmed. Osburn also admits that he was "too tired to take note of all that was happening, and may have given some of the events in their wrong order."[13] So Bridges' "harangue" may have been the one he was to give later in the town square.

The existence of the surrender document was now exercising Mainwaring:

> I said I must get the paper back from the Mayor. The cavalry officers said they meant to have that. I said I did not mind who had it as long as it was recovered. The cavalry subaltern accompanied me to the Mairie, and, pushing on in front, demanded the paper. I was too proud to argue with him for possession of it, as I was still upheld with the conviction that I had done my duty. They took it and sent it to their General.[14]

Bridges set about requisitioning carts to carry those soldiers who simply could not march a step further and assembled as many men as possible in the square. The sound of stray shots could be heard in other parts of the town and Osburn speculated that, while it might be a few drunken soldiers shooting at shadows, "did some of Bridges's [sic] squadron shoot a few who too truculently scorned their suggestion that there was still time to run and fight another day?"[15]

In the square Bridges had to get the men to their feet:

> There was a toy-shop handy which provided my trumpeter and myself with a tin whistle and a drum and we marched round and round the fountain where the men were lying like the dead playing the British Grenadiers and Tipperary and beating the drum like mad. They sat up and began to laugh and even cheer. I stopped playing and made them a short exhortation and told them I was going to take them back to their regiments. They began to stand up and fall in.[16]

Back at the station, and presumably after Bridges's ultimatum, Mainwaring:

> told the men the situation had changed, and called upon them to follow me. After a couple of minutes they fell in, got their arms and ammunition, filled their water-bottles, and awaited orders.[17]

Once the whole ragged force had been assembled in the square Bridges asked Osburn to sort them into fours and count them: there were 440 men and of these approximately 200 are believed to have been men of the Royal Warwickshire and Royal Dublin Fusiliers.

Mainwaring says that they set off at 9pm:

> only to be again halted for another hour in the town. This was my fourth night without sleep, and twice I fell down when standing up.[18]

Osburn recollected that the thickset Mainwaring:

> looked very pale, entirely dazed, had no Sam Browne belt, and leant heavily on his stick, apparently so exhausted with fatigue and heat that he could scarcely have known what he was doing. Some of his men called to him encouraging words, affectionate and familiar, but not meant insolently - such as 'Buck up, sir! Cheer up, daddy! Now we shan't be long! We are all going back to 'Hang-le-Tear'![19]

While Mainwaring states that they finally moved off at 10pm, Osburn says it was not until at least half past midnight that they left St. Quentin. Both describe how the commandeered wagons were filled to overflowing with the footsore men. Osburn continues:

> So through the darkness and the thick shrouding fog of that summer night we marched out, literally feeling our way through the countryside, so thick was the mist.[20]

They got out just in time. Before leaving St. Quentin Osburn had had to return to the deserted Grande Place to collect a forgotten map case and "heard an ominous sound - the metallic rattle on the cobbles of cavalry in formation entering the town through one of the darkened side streets that led into the Grande Place."[21] It seems likely that, this time at least, these were Uhlans, men of *Ulanen-Regiment 16*, the divisional cavalry of *VII. Armeekorps.*[22]

Mainwaring describes how the column:

> moved very slowly, with a cavalry escort, and about 2a.m. halted at a farm and village named Roupy. Here the cavalry left us, and after blocking the road by putting the waggons across it, and posting picquets on it, I lay down and slept till dawn, the first sleep I had been able to get since Monday morning.

> Friday. Aug. 28th - Soon after daybreak the cavalry rejoined us, and escorted us some way, till, telling us to make for St. Surplice [Sulpice], they left us. I must say here that before the two officers withdrew both of them shook hands with me, and said I had done everything a man could do.

> We marched all that day, coming up with the 3rd Division, until, at

evening, we reached Noyan [Noyon], where we were entrained and taken to Compiegne.

This concludes Mainwaring's account of his part in the affair of the two colonels.

As to Elkington, he is known to have left St. Quentin alone, but why, exactly how far in advance of Bridges and Mainwaring, and to what destination is not known. It is known that Lieutenant C.P. Cowper, the Warwickshire Special Reserve officer who had accompanied Mainwaring and Elkington to St. Quentin, and the Warwickshire other ranks, found their way to Ham and were there entrained for Compiègne.

On 28th August, according to the War Diary of the 1/R. Warwickshire, Elkington, Major C. Christie and 280 men, rejoined the 10th Brigade in the area of Voyennes/Bussy. There is no indication of when Mainwaring or Elkington were placed under arrest or were charged with "Behaving in a scandalous manner unbecoming the character of an officer and a gentleman."

10
The Clarke/Trigona Party

We left Major Shewan and his column in the dawn light of 27th August, advancing cautiously along the road from Ligny to Clary. The advance guard was found by A Company, 2/R. Dublin Fusiliers (Captain N.P. Clarke) with two platoons under Captain A.S. Trigona leading. The road ran south-east through flat beet fields and after about three-quarters of a mile the column crossed the track of a meandering narrow gauge light railway that to the right of the road ran on a slight embankment; to the left of the road was a farm building. About 600 yards further on, on the right of the road, was a disused distillery.

The main body of the column had reached the distillery when there was firing from ahead, where Captain Trigona's two platoons were in view of Clary. The main body took cover at the distillery and through binoculars Captain Trigona could be seen signalling towards Clary while his men were lying down in extended order facing the village.

A party of uniformed men could be seen at the entrance of the village and from the position occupied by Shewan and Clarke those uniforms *"looked British."*[1] Captain Higginson, commanding the rearguard, now came up and, agreeing with the identification of the friendly troops, said he would go ahead and tell Trigona to push on.

The main body was re-formed on the road and as they marched forward a cyclist[2] was sent on towards the village to tell the troops there not to fire on their own people.

Trigona was still not convinced that the men in the village were British. After the initial burst of fire the "villagers" had signalled to the advancing troops in English "what regiment is that?", to which Trigona had signalled back "Dublin Fusiliers." This had brought the response "Good; come on, Dublin Fusiliers." Unconvinced by this exchange Trigona then signalled "Will you send out a man?" A man duly appeared and advanced about 50 yards before dropping prone. Trigona remained unconvinced.

The initial outburst of firing had wounded three of the advance guard's five man "point," and they all now lay some yards ahead of Trigona. At first they too thought that it was a case of mistaken identity and that they had been fired on by British troops. However, the unwounded NCO commanding the "point" quickly came to the conclusion that the enemy held the village and as the cyclist pedalled up to where he lay the NCO called out for him to stop. The cyclist didn't halt and the NCO yelled after him, "Come back, come back, they're Germans." The unheeding cyclist pedalled on and was quite close to the village when a single aimed shot carried him off the cycle and dumped him on the road, a huddled and unmoving bundle of khaki.

This shot was the signal for an outbreak of sustained rifle and machine-gun fire from the enemy in concealed positions along the margins of the village to the front and right front of the Dublin Fusiliers whose advance guard returned fire as the main body extended into the beet fields to the right of the road and sought cover.

> But although there was a good deal of cover from view there was no cover from fire, and the bullets swished and stung through those roots in a very nasty way.[3]

The driver of the machine-gun wagon was shot and the two horses, maddened by the firing, dragged the wagon into a field and then out again and then down the road to Ligny, taking with them the machine-gun that Major Shewan had been at such pains to bring away from Haucourt.

Shewan now ordered his men to fall back, first to the disused distillery, then to the farm building where the light railway crossed the road. Small parties of men dashed back, mutually supporting one another with rifle fire.

> The rattle of musketry increased, and the bullets came whizzing and flipping amongst them. The men spread out as they ran for greater safety. But in spite of all this, it wasn't always nice to watch a rush. One was forcibly reminded of rabbits being bolted. ... A retirement under fire is always nasty - this was positively horrid. And yet, as I watched those men running and falling, I felt convinced that the losses were not as heavy as they seemed, and that in some cases a man slipped on the wet dewy turnip[s] and fell sideways and then lay doggo, but that he was not hit.[4]

From the embankment the survivors fell back on Ligny where the wounded they had managed to carry away with them were added to those already in the church. Germans were now reported to be approaching from Haucourt and Clary and the survivors therefore moved north towards Caudry. The party had been reduced from around 400 strong to only thirty men led by two officers, Captain Clarke and Captain Trigona.

The action on the road to Clary had resulted in the death of one officer, 2nd-Lieutenant J.G.M. Dunlop, and in six others being captured: Major H.M. Shewan (wounded), Captain G.S. Higginson (wounded), Lieutenant J.E. Vernon (wounded), Lieutenant C.H.L'E. West (wounded), Lieutenant J.F.K. Dobbs and 2nd Lieutenant F.C.S. Macky. Some 44 other ranks were killed in action or died of wounds received that day. A large number, both wounded and unwounded, were captured.

The Clarke/Trigona party moved off the road to Caudry and struck out across country and down into the valley of the Warnelle, following the line of a ditch beside the embankment of the railway line to Cambrai and collecting small groups of other stragglers as they went. At about 8.30am they found a well-concealed hiding place and halted for the day. It was explained to the men by Clarke:

> that our object was to rejoin as soon as possible, and not to fight, for if
> we indulged in fighting there was small hope of ever rejoining, and any
> fighting we could do would not help the general operations. They were
> further told that we must continue to march westward until we were
> outside the German right wing, when we would turn south, but that
> whilst in the enemy's lines we must rest by day and march by night.[5]

Moreover, their best route lay round the north of Cambrai.

Their hideout was on the previous day's battlefield, about midway between Fontaine-au-Pire and Haucourt, and they watched as the local farmworkers moved over the ground collecting the wounded. They cautiously left hiding to gather up discarded emergency rations to augment their own meagre supplies and contacted one of the Frenchmen:

> He arranged to send us some water, and told us there were four
> Englishmen in hiding close by. These four men came down during the
> day. They recounted various adventures. One had been captured and
> escaped. They were all in mufti, and wanted to join our party. As their
> uniform was not far off, they were told they would be allowed to join if
> they came in uniform, not otherwise. So they brought over their uniform
> during the day and changed in the ditch, becoming soldiers once more.[6]

For the night they moved to some entrenchments on the edge of a cornfield and they were still there at midday on the 28th when two wandering German soldiers, ambulatory patients from a nearby field hospital, stumbled into them. Clarke and Trigona questioned them, had them blindfolded and when the party moved on their hands were tied behind them and they were left beside the railway.

Their next unwelcome encounter was with a German medical officer and his orderly, out searching for their missing patients. Clarke, who apparently spoke fluent German, persuaded the doctor to give his word of honour not to give them away and let him and the orderly go. Clarke had "every reason to believe that this officer kept his word."[7]

The party went back to the ditch and waited for nightfall when they moved west to Longsart and then north across country hoping to strike the Cambrai railway between Wambaix and Cattenières. They eventually found an unguarded bridge, crossed to the north of the line and hid again, waiting for the dawn of 29th August.

Fearing imminent discovery by German search parties they moved on in the morning fog, passing Cattenières on the left, crossed the Cambrai-Le Cateau road slightly east of Igniel and pushed on cross country towards Carnières:

> ...when suddenly the fog lifted and we got the shock of our lives... About 600-800 yards away to our left ran the Igmel [Igniel]-Carnières road, and this road was covered as far as we could see (about half a mile perhaps) with a column of infantry and transport marching in the opposite direction.

> Mounted officers rode at their head. I think the Germans were as surprised as we were. Both forces instantly halted ... An examination through glasses showed that they were looking at us in the same way, with the mounted officers talking together, and all the troops in the column gazing at us. ...

> We had not halted probably for more than 15-20 seconds when the order was given to move on, and in the same close formation (column of route). We pushed along, all eyes glued to the left, wondering when the first shot was coming from that long, silent, hostile column, or when a horse was going to come galloping across to find out what and who we were. It seemed impossible that they could let us go without question.[8]

Amazingly, the Germans simply marched on, bluffed into believing the British troops were German, just as the Germans had bluffed the Dublin Fusiliers three days earlier.

Near Carnières they went into hiding in a cornfield, where they remained all day. They again made contact with local inhabitants and obtained food and information. Moreover, they were able to work out a system whereby they would be able to obtain food and information each day.

"Whenever we halted we would tell certain local inhabitants the direction in which we next wanted to go, and they would send out cyclists to discover the German dispositions in that area."[9] They would then devise a route based on this local information and move on to hiding places found for them by "certain local inhabitants," who were most probably priests.

Their move during the night of 29/30th August was across country to Naves on the Cambrai - Bavai road and thence across the Cambrai-Denain road to woods near the Canal de L'Escaut in the vicinity of Thun-Leveque. During the night they had increased their strengh by eight Gordon Highlanders "who had somehow detached from their battalion and had lain hidden for three days."[10]

They hid in the woods throughout 30th August and came very close to being discovered by German troops on a number of occasions. That night, with the help of a civilian guide, they moved on to Fressies, beside the Sensée river/canal, and concealed themselves in an empty house. During the evening of 31st August their civilian guide reported that the bridges at Aubigny were temporarily unguarded, so they risked a crossing in the twilight and marched on through the night to Erchin. The following night they marched west, to avoid Douai, via Goeulzin, Estrées and Vitry en Artois, before turning north to pass through Izel-lez-Equerchin and on to a halting place at about 2.30am on 2nd September. "This was a march of about sixteen miles, and included the crossing of [the] Douai-Cambrai main road, the Sensée Canal, and the Douai-Arras road."[11]

The party was now on the very fringe of the right flank of the German advance and felt able to relax just a little. Their presence became known to an ever increasing number of local farmworkers who brought them not only food and water but also news of German movements and dispositions. On hearing that they wanted to move generally south-west to get well beyond the German flank, a local car owner drove Clarke into Lens where he was able to arrange for passage on a light railway that ran from Lens to Frevent, leaving at 7.20 the next morning.

That night they moved closer to Lens and at 5am on 3rd September they marched cautiously into its southern outskirts just as the Germans were reportedly entering from the north. They found their train already full of the latest group of reservists who, regardless of the approach of the Germans, were going off to report to their depots. Room was found for the British and they clattered and rumbled south-west and reached Frevent, some 8 miles south of St. Pol, at about 11am.

In Frevent they met a British officer on reconnaissance in a car:

> He said that when he came into Frevent and heard that we were there, he couldn't believe it, and thought it must be a German force that was there. He told us we could never get south, as the Germans were south of Amiens, and well west of it. So we should have to go round by sea. He promised to get instructions for us by telephone at Abbeville, where he was returning.[12]

Meanwhile, they should march south-west to Auxi-le-Chateau (about nine miles) and he would send back wagons from Abbeville to meet them there.

They reached Auxi at dusk and "were very kindly treated and fed, and given a good hall with plenty of straw to sleep on."[13] The wagons duly arrived the next morning, 4th September, and carried them safely to Abbeville. "They were in five waggons, and the procession looked like a school treat, for every waggon was decorated with bouquets of flowers given the men by women and children as they came through the country."[14]

Since it was thought that the railway line between Abbeville and Amiens had been cut their only option was to travel north by train along the coast to Boulogne, which they reached that evening. On 5th September they were shipped back to England and a few days later were drafted back to their regiments in France.

Clarke estimated that the "distance covered from the scene of action to Abbeville was about 125 miles, of which 35 miles were by light railway." The party that reached Abbeville comprised the following:15

Officers -
Captain N.P. Clarke, 2/R, Dublin Fusiliers
Captain A.S. Trigona, 2/R, Dublin Fusiliers

N.C.O.s and Men -

Royal Scots	3
King's Own Regiment	3
Royal Warwickshire	5
Somerset Light Infantry	8
West Riding Regiment	1
East Lancashire Regiment	2

Hampshire Regiment	5
Gordon Highlanders	8
Royal Irish Fusiliers	4
Munster Fusiliers	2
Royal Dublin Fusiliers	35
	76

*   *   *

It will be remembered that Major Poole of the Warwickshire and his party spent the night of 26th August in a village that the following morning they discovered was Caullery. "Roused at the first signs of dawn we fell in in a street, and just as we moved off Major [R.G.] Parker, The King's Own and his party appeared but took another route and we only met them once again during the morning."[16]

The Poole party, which included Lieutenant B.L. Montgomery, moved south to Elincourt and with bodies of German troops to be seen off to the east they marched west to Malincourt and then headed south-west via Villers Outréaux to Gouy. During this march they picked up an officer and private of the 1/Gordon Highlanders "who had been taken prisoners but succeeded in effecting their escape, both declared that they were the sole survivors of their company - they were without arms or equipment."[17] There was also a close call with a German cavalry patrol moving only a few hundred yards ahead of them as they passed through one village.

It was at Gouy that Poole decided to hide the machine-guns: "I considered it absolutely necessary to leave the guns as the men were physically incapable of carrying them further."[18] Lieutenant C.C. Bamber, the Warwickshire Machine-gun Officer, buried them in the garden of a house in Gouy. The spare parts were hidden in another place, close by.[19] From Gouy they marched to Bony and from there to Ronssoy, where they lay up in a wood during the afternoon while a cavalry action went on nearby.

"The men had been instructed to keep under cover in the wood but one man went off to forage and was seen to be pounced on by some Uhlans - a punishment for his disobedience."[20] Poole decided to move the party before they were all rounded up and they managed to slip away through Hargicourt to a little beyond Hesbecourt where they settled down in a sunken lane. They contacted a villager and arranged to send back two parties, one to collect bread and the other water.

Both parties returned in haste and empty handed when Uhlans were spotted nearby. Later, their friendly villager turned up:

> with a supply of only some two dozen hoop like loaves and a pot of conserve from his wife for the officers. The bread did not go far with our party but it was the best that could be done. The pangs of hunger, the footsoreness and the weariness of ten hours marching, during which we had covered some 25 miles, were forgotten in sleep.[21]

Very early the next morning, 28th August, they marched through Jeancourt and then across country to Bernes where they arrived at 7am:

> Here we halted and commandeered all the bread to be had which may have worked out at about 1/4lb per man and the men were able to get some coffee.[22]

On the advice of a French staff officer they moved off towards Péronne and became entangled with some manoeuvring French cavalry, "looking most picturesque in their variously coloured uniforms," before moving on.

> Later, we came to a place where someone had dumped rations and there were several quarters of beef, boxes of sugar and biscuits, the first and only sign we had seen to show us we were in the tracks of our own people.

> We did not halt, but as I went along I picked up as many biscuits as I could and handed them to the men, who gladly accepted them, and to their credit be it said not a man broke the ranks to help himself, in spite of the fact that they had been so many hours with so little food and many must have been very hungry. A fine example of good discipline.[23]

They marched on and reached Matigny at about 2pm, when they:

> beheld for us the glorious sight of British infantry at work on some defences. A long halt was made to gather in the tail of stragglers and then we moved on in company with some artillery, reaching the bridges over the Somme, river and canal, which we crossed hardly an hour before they were blown up. We chanced to meet our Staff Captain who directed us to a farm which we reached in about an hour, after passing through a rear guard in position. Here we had a couple of hours' rest, a little food and a much needed wash and bathing of painful feet.[24]

They marched on with the rear-guard of the 4th Division but were unable to keep up. First they were picked up and carried aboard some empty supply wagons and were then transferred to lorries to be carried on to Noyon. Here they "slept the night in a ditch" and the following morning, 29th August, went on to Compiègne where there was "a large camp containing 3,000 men, stragglers and lost men of numerous units, some with and some without officers. Here we found an officer and some men of the 1st R. Warwickshire Regt."[25]

Slowly, the stragglers, the lost, the confused, and the weary, were sorted out and many moved on to Le Mans where units that were able to muster at least 100 men were allowed to rejoin their brigades. Fourteen officers and 402 men under Major Poole rejoined the remnants of the 1/R. Warwickshire at Brie Compte Robert on 5th September, the last day of the Retreat from Mons. Montgomery considered Poole a "first class regimental officer" and that "it was due entirely to him that we finally got back to the British Expeditionary Force and joined up with our battalion."[26]

By 13th September the 1/R. Warwickshire could muster 17 officers and 775 other ranks, while the 2/R. Dublin Fusiliers had only 10 officers and 478 other ranks and could form only three weak companies. It would be many weeks before either battalion recovered to its full strength. In other ways they did not recover at all.

11

"Conduct unbecoming..."
The General Court Martial of the Colonels
Elkington's Redemption

The General Court Martial of Lieut.-Colonel A.E. Mainwaring and Lieut.-Colonel J.F. Elkington was held at Chouy on 12th September 1914. Both officers were charged with "'Behaving in a scandalous manner unbecoming the character of an officer and a gentleman,' in that they, at St. Quentin, on 27th August 1914, during a retirement following upon an engagement at Ligny, without due cause, agreed together to surrender themselves and the troops under their respective command."

The President of the GCM was Br.-General A.G. Hunter-Weston, commander of the 11th Infantry Brigade, 4th Division, his fellow members of the court being, it is said, five full colonels. The case for the prosecution was presented by the Deputy Judge Advocate-General, J.G.S. Mellor, Esq.[1] Apparently the proceedings were brief, the defence case being simply that, in attemping to surrender, the two colonels had been motivated solely by the desire to prevent unnecessary loss of civilian life. The verdict of the court on both officers was "Guilty" and both were sentenced "to be cashiered." The sentence was immediately confirmed by the Commander-in-Chief and both the charge and sentence were promulgated as Army Routine Order 88 of 14th September 1914. The sentences alone were published in the *London Gazette* on 30th October 1914, leading to brief press notices the following day.

Mainwaring was 50 years old and sick when he was returned to England in disgrace. Exactly where he went and how he spent the next fifteen years is largely unclear. One source suggests that he enlisted in the Middlesex Regiment and was killed in action during the winter of 1917. It is just possible that he attemped to enlist and may have succeeded, but it seems very unlikely. He was certainly not killed in action during the war.

At some point, while the war was still in progress, he wrote and had privately printed and distributed an *apologia* in the form of an 8-page pamphlet, *A Statement* [by] *A.E.M.*, prefaced with this comment: "This Statement is made for my friends, of whom I find there are many more than I thought. I rely on my friends not to use it to try and get any redress for me until Peace has been declared." It also has an epilogue:

> What the men think of the matter may be judged from the following extract from a letter from an Officer in my late regiment, who, unsolicited by me, is collecting evidence in the hope that it may be of use when peace is declared:
>
> 'There is not a man here that does not believe implicitly in you and what you did to save them. There are several men in the other regiments now who swear that you alone saved them, so I am collecting as much information as possible which will assist in bringing things to light when this show is over.'

The information thus collected by the unnamed officer does not seem to have survived and only one copy of Mainwaring's *Statement* has come to light so far. Apparently there was no post-war effort to obtain redress for Mainwaring. Perhaps the example of Elkington's wartime rehabilitation and the manner in which it was achieved obscured a more measured peacetime effort on behalf of Mainwaring.

In January 1927 Mainwaring and his wife were living in Melbourne, Derbyshire, and it may have been here that he suffered the stroke that paralysed him down one side. By the autumn of 1930 they had moved to Pounsley Mill, Blackboys, Framfield, East Sussex, and it was here, on 11th October 1930, that Arthur Edward Mainwaring, aged 66, died of a heart attack, aggravated by the stroke, chronic asthma and persistent high blood pressure.

In death there was at least a small measure of posthumous rehabilitation, his death certificate describing him as a "Retired Lieut. Colonel Royal Dublin Fusiliers."

                    *   *   *

When Elkington was returned to England in September 1914 it is clear that he had already made up his mind as to his only course of action. He spent a few days with his newly born daughter, and putting his affairs in order and making his farewells. He then travelled to Paris and enlisted in the French Foreign Legion. He was inducted as a

Légionnaire 2nd Class number 29274 and probably served with the *2ᵉ régiment de marche* of the *1ᵉʳ étranger* and certainly took part in the attack on Hill 140 (Vimy Ridge) on 9th May 1915, in which the Legion lost 1,889 men, some 50 per cent of the strength of the attacking battalions. He was also present for the attack on Hill 119 at Souchez on 16th June 1915, when the Legion again sustained heavy losses.

During his sevice in the Legion Elkington was recognised only once: "we were marching in the Champagne country, and had just stopped to drink at a stream when a military motor went by. Someone in the car called out 'Hullo, Elkington', and I was afraid I would be given away." But the moment passed and the convention that a Legionnaire did not have to speak of his life before the Legion was not threatened.

He made friends with a medical officer, an American named Wheeler, who had originally joined the French Red Coss and then, having tired of that, had transferred to the Foreign Legion. On 28th September 1915 they were in the same wave of the attack by the *2ᵉ régiment de marche* of the *1ᵉʳ étranger* on Navarin Farm, when the Legion lost 2,003 officers and men, killed, wounded, and missing. Among the wounded were Elkington and Dr. Wheeler, both caught in the legs and lower body by the same burst of machine-gun fire. Elkington's right leg was dreadfully smashed, Wheeler's legs not much less so. Wheeler tended Elkington's and his own wounds and gave Elkington a "stiff dose of laudnum." Of Elkington's mangled leg he managed to say, "I say, old man, they will have to take that off," before fainting across it.

They lay out for 13 hours, about 100 yards short of the German second line trenches, before being picked up by a French patrol. Wheeler survived his wounds, though crippled for life, and was awarded the *Croix de Guerre*. For Elkington, taken to a hospital in Grenoble, it was touch and go for a long time. He was operated on eight times by a skilled military surgeon, Major Termier, with the result that his leg was saved. He spent many months in hospital and whilst there he was awarded the *Medaille Militaire* and *Croix de Guerre avec Palme*.

On discharge from the Foreign Legion and from hospital Elkington returned to England to complete his convalescence. The story of his recovery of his honour through gallant service against the common foe was brought to the notice of the President of his Court Martial, Lieut.-General Sir Aylmer Hunter-Weston, now commanding VIII Corps in France. In July 1916 Hunter-Weston wrote to Elkington, not only to congratulate him on his gallant and gentlemanly behaviour in regaining his honour in the ranks of the Foreign Legion, but also to say that he had had an interview with the Adjutant-General to the Forces, Lieut.-General C.F.N. Macready, to see what could be done to obtain a pardon. At the end of August he wrote again to Elkington to say that a pardon and reinstatement would be forthcoming. However, when the notice appeared in the *London Gazette* and *The Times* on 7th September 1916, it stated only that: "the King has approved of the reinstatement of John Ford Elkington in the rank of Lieutenant-Colonel, with his previous seniority, in consequence of his gallant conduct while serving in the ranks of the Foreign Legion of the French Army." Obviously, it would not have been possible to pardon Elkington without doing the same for Mainwaring, as they had been jointly charged at their Court Martial.

On 20th October Elkington - "still very lame, but is otherwise in good health" - was received by the King and on 28th October the following notice appeared in the *London Gazette*:

"His Majesty the King has been graciously pleased to appoint Lieutenant-Colonel John Ford Elkington, Royal Warwickshire Regiment, to be a Companion of the Distinguished Service Order."

Elkington's wound did not permit him any further service. He went on half pay in February 1918, retired in July 1919, and settled at Adbury Holt, Newbury, Berkshire, with his family that now included his daughter, Jean Margaret Rew, born 9th September 1914, and a younger son, Richard Ford Rew, born 22nd May 1918.

In 1939 Jean Elkington married Lieut.-Colonel Sir William Richard de Bacquencourt Des Voeux, Grenadier Guards, by whom she had three daughters. Her husband was killed in action at Arnhem on 20th September 1944, whilst commanding 156th Battalion, Parachute Regiment (Anti-Aircraft) and is buried at Oosterbeek.

Elkington's elder son, John, served with the Rifle Brigade in North Africa and Italy, attained the rank of Lieut.-Colonel and was awarded the OBE.

Richard Elkington joined the Territorials in 1938 and was serving as a Captain with the 10/Rifle Brigade in Tunisia when he received wounds from which he died on 19th January 1943. He is buried in the Medjez-el-Bab War Cemetery, Tunisia.[2]

Lieut.-Colonel John Ford Elkington, DSO, died on 27th June 1944. He and his younger son, Richard, are jointly commemorated in Burghclere Church, Hampshire, by a memorial window unveiled at the dedication service by an old family friend, Field-Marshal Lord Montgomery, whose own memories of Le Cateau and August 1914 must have been particularly strong that day; perhaps he was particularly grateful not to have memories of St. Quentin on 27th August 1914.

Appendix I

4th Division Order of Battle

10th Infantry Brigade
1st The Royal Warwickshire Regiment
2nd Seaforth Highlanders
1st Princess Victoria's (Royal Irish Rifles)
2nd The Royal Dublin Fusiliers

11th Infantry Brigade
1st Prince Albert's (Somerset Light Infantry)
1st The East Lancashire Regiment
1st The Hampshire Regiment
1st Rifle Brigade

12th Infantry Brigade
1st King's Own
2nd The Lancashire Fusiliers
2nd The Royal Inniskilling Fusiliers
2nd The Essex Regiment

Divisional Troops

(Those in brackets [ ] had not joined the division by 26th August 1914, the Battle of Le Cateau).

Mounted Troops
[B Sqdn. 19th Hussars; 4th Cyclist Company]

Artillery
XIV Brigade RFA, 39th, 68th and 88th Batteries, XIV Brigade Ammunition Column;
XXIX Brigade RFA, 125th, 126th and 127th Batteries, XXIX Brigade Ammunition Column;
XXXII Brigade RFA, 27th, 134th and 135th Batteries, XXXII Brigade Ammunition Column;
XXXVII (Howitzer) Brigade RFA, 31st, 35th and 55th (Howitzer) Batteries, XXXVII (Howitzer) Brigade Ammunition Column;
[31st Heavy Battery RGA and Heavy Battery Ammunition Column];
[4th Divisional Ammunition Column]

Engineers
[7th Field Company and 9th Field Company RE]

Signal Services
[4th Signal Company]

Divisional Train
[4th Divisional Train (18, 25, 32 and 38 Coys. ASC)]

Medical Units
[10th, 11th and 12th Field Ambulances]

Veterinary Section
4th Mobile Veterinary Section

Appendix II

4th Division Staff

Commander   Major-General T.D'O. Snow, CB
Aide-de-Camp to Commander   Captain H.I.R. Allfrey, SLI
Aide-de-Camp to Commander   Captain P.O.E. D'Estterre, ELR

General Staff Branch

GSO1   Colonel J.E. Edmonds, CB, RE
GSO2   Lieut.-Colonel A.A. Montgomery, RA
GSO3   Captain E.T. Humphreys, Lancashire Fusiliers

Adjutant and Quarter Master-General's Branch

Assistant A&QMG   Lieut.-Col. F.P.S. Taylor, ASC
Deputy Assistant A&QMG   Captain B.F. Burnett Hitchcock,
Notts. & Derby Regt.
Deputy Assistant QMG   Captain H.J. Elles, RE

Administrative Service and Departments

Assistant Director of Medical Services   Colonel C.E. Faunce,
RAMC
Deputy ADMS   Major H. Ensor, DSO, MB, RAMC
Assistant Director of Veterinary Services   Major R.H. Holmes,
FRCVS, AVC
Deputy Assistant Director of Ordnance Services   Major
O.B. Harter, DLI
Field Cashier   Major C.V. Isacke, Army Pay Dept.

Special Appointment

Assistant Provost-Marshal   Lieut. F.A. Atchison,
Hampshire Regt.

HQ Divisional Artillery

Commander	Br.-General G.F. Milne, CB, DSO, RA
ADC to Commander	Captain O.M. Lanyon, RA
Brigade-Major	Captain E.H.G. Leggett, RA
Staff Captain	Captain C.A.L. Graham, RA

HQ Divisional Engineers

Commander	Lieut.-Colonel H.B. Jones, RE
Adjutant	Captain W.G.S. Dobbie, RE

10th Brigade

Commander	Br.-General J.A.L. Haldane, CB, DSO
Brigade-Major	Major F.E.Ll. Daniell, Seaforths
Staff Captain	Captain T.H.C. Frankland, Dublins

11th Brigade

Commander	Br.-General A.G. Hunter-Weston, CB, DSO
Brigade-Major	Captain G.F. Boyd, DSO, Leinsters
Staff Captain	Captain W.H.M. Freestun, SLI

12th Brigade

Commander	Br.-General H.F.M. Wilson, CB
Brigade-Major	Captain C.M. Davies, Rifle Brigade
Staff Captain	Captain O.H. North, Lancashire Fusiliiers

Appendix III

Officers of 1st Battalion, The Royal Warwickshire Regiment, August 1914

Lieut.-Colonel J.F. Elkington
Major A.J. Poole
Major W.C. Christie
Major D.A.L. Day
Major R.F.Meiklejohn, DSO
Captain P.E. Besant
Captain H.C. Sinnott
Captain C.F. Burnard
Captain R. Wood
Captain J.A.M. Bannerman (Adjutant)
Captain C.T. Tomes
Captain E.V.M. Shelley
Captain C.A.C. Bentley
Captain H.C. Hart
Lieutenant C.G.P. Gilliat
Lieutenant J.H.W. Knight-Bruce (Depot)
Lieutenant B.L. Montgomery
Lieutenant C.C. Bamber
Lieutenant H.J.I. Walker
Lieutenant O.A. Knapton
Lieutenant C.F. Maunsell
Lieutenant C.W.C. Wasey
Lieutenant A.H.K. Jackson
Lieutenant C.P. Cowper (Special Reserve)
2nd Lieutenant C.H.J. Chichester-Constable
2nd Lieutenant J.T. Bretherton
2nd Lieutenant E.V. Briscoe
2nd Lieutenant C.E. Dalton
2nd Lieutenant R.B.B. Tillyer
Captain & Qmr. T.H. Harwood

Officers of 2nd Battalion, The Royal Dublin Fusiliers, August 1914

Lieut.-Colonel A.E. Mainwaring
Major H.M. Shewan, DSO
Captain G.S. Higginson
Captain N.P. Clarke
Captain R.L.H. Conlan
Captain S.G.deC. Wheeler
Captain W.H. Supple
Captain A.S. Trigona
Captain R.M. Watson (Adjutant)
Lieutenant J.E. Vernon
Lieutenant J.F.K. Dobbs
Lieutenant T.J. Leahy
Lieutenant C.H.L'E. West
Lieutenant W.H. Braddell
Lieutenant R.F.H. Massy-Westropp
2nd Lieutenant J. MacN. Dickie
2nd Lieutenant F.C.S. Macky
2nd Lieutenant B. Maguire
2nd Lieutenant J.G.M. Dunlop
2nd Lieutenant R.A.J. Goff
2nd Lieutenant W.M. Robinson
Captain & Qmr. J. Burke

Notes

Introduction (page vi)

1. Kingsford (C.L.) *The Story of the Royal Warwickshire Regiment* ("Country Life," [1921]); Wylly (Col. H.C.) *Crown and Company: The Historical Records of the 2nd Battalion Royal Dublin Fusiliers*, Vol. 2: *1911-1922* (Gale & Polden, Aldershot, [1923]); Haldane (General Sir Aylmer) *A Brigade of the Old Army* (Edward Arnold, 1920).

2. Osburn (Arthur) *Unwilling Passenger* (Faber & Faber, 1932); Bridges (Lt.-Gen. Sir Tom) *Alarms & Excursions* (Longmans, 1938); Hill (Pte. R.G.) "An Old Contemptible at Le Cateau" in *Everyman at War*, ed. C.B. Purdom (Dent, 1930).

3. Macdonald (Lyn) *1914* (Michael Joseph, 1987). As regards the "two colonels" this particular work is chiefly remarkable for the footnote concerning them that appears on p.198. Virtually every "fact" is incorrect and a curiously distorted version of the later career of Elkington (consistently misspelt Ellington) is bestowed on Mainwaring. See also Caffrey (Kate) *Farewell Leicester Square: The Old Contemptibles, 12 August-19 November 1914* (Andre Deutsch, 1980) and Travers (Tim) *The Killing Ground: The British Army, the Western Front and the Emergence of Modern Warfare 1900-1918* (Allen & Unwin, 1987).

Chapter 1 (pages 1-9)

1. Edmonds (Br.-Gen. Sir J.E.) Contrib. to *The Dictionary of National Biography 1931-1940* (OUP, 1949). As regards the Standing Orders, Snow recalled: "Colonel Edmonds and Captain Burnett-Hitchcock had just completed our war standing orders, a most complete volume which was of great value. These orders had been published in the previous winter and were so good that the 3rd, 5th and 6th Division adopted them at once and later most of the Service Battalion and the Territorial Battalion standing orders were taken from them." Snow (General T.D'O.) *Account of the Retreat of 1914*, p.2. PRO: CAB 45/129.

2. Falls (Capt. Cyril) contrib. to *The Dictionary of National Biography 1951-1960* (OUP, 1971).

3. Snow (General T.D'O) *Account of the Retreat of 1914*, p.2. PRO: CAB 45/129

4. Snow, ibid, pp. 3-4

5. Snow, ibid, p.4.

6. Haldane (Br.-Gen. J.A.L.) *[Shorncliffe diary]*, 13th March 1913. IWM.

7. Haldane, ibid, 3rd May 1913

8. Snow's confidential report quoted in Haldane, ibid, 1st December 1913. An officer always saw his annual confidential report, indeed he was instructed to "initial the report at the place assigned for the purpose to show that he has seen it." - *The Kings Regulations and Orders for the Army*, 1912, para. 133.

9. Douglas's confidential report quoted in Haldane, ibid, 14th April 1913.

10. Haldane, ibid, 4th July 1913

11. Grierson's confidential report quoted in Haldane, ibid, 1st December 1913.

12. Chichester (Henry Manners) contrib. to *The Dictionary of National Biography*.

13. Haldane, ibid, 11th and 24th July 1913. "Churcher ... was a complete failure in the field from the beginning of the war and a danger to his battalion when under fire." Haldane, ibid, Postscript. With Smith- Dorrien's approval Haldane

had Churcher removed from his command at 3am on 5th September, 1914. Churcher spent the rest of the war in various staff appointments in coastal defences and garrisons. He retired in January 1920.

14. Haldane, ibid, 10th April 1913.

15. Haldane, ibid, 12th January 1914.

16. Haldane, ibid. 15th May 1913.

17. Haldane, ibid, 24th May 1913.

18. Haldane, ibid, 31st October 1913.

19. Haldane, ibid, 25th April 1913.

20. General Sir Cecil Francis Romer, GCB, KBE, CMG, DL (1869-1962). Served in various staff appointments 1914-1917 and commanded the 59th Division in France, April 1917 - June 1918.

21. See *Sources*, below, for bibliographical details.

22. Haldane (General Sir J.A.L.) *A Soldier's Saga* (Blackwood, 1948) p. [278].

23. Haldane, *[Shorncliffe diary]*, Postscript.

Chapter 2 (pages 11-17)

1. Snow, op. cit., p.4.

2. Hamilton (Nigel) *Monty: The Making of a General 1887-1942* (Hamish Hamilton, 1981) p.64.

3. Hazlehurst (Cameron) *Politicians at War* (Cape, 1971) p.101.

4. Williamson (Samuel R.) *The Politics of Grand Strategy* (Harvard University Press, 1969) p.312. See also PRO: WO 33/665.

5. Hill (R.G.) in *Everyman at War*, ed. C.B. Purdom (Dent, 1930) p.10

6. Hill, ibid, p.10.

7. Knight-Bruce (Lt. J.H.W.) PRO: CAB 45/196.

8. Montgomery (Field-Marshal The Viscount) *The Memoirs* (Collins, 1958) pp. 31-32.

9. Williamson, op. cit., p.310.

10. Williamson, op. cit., p.310.

11. The 6th Division did not begin to disembark at St. Nazaire until 6th September 1914.

12. Haldane (Lt.-Gen.J.A.L.) *A Brigade of the Old Army* (Edward Arnold, 1920) p.1.

13. Haldane, *[Shorncliffe Diary]*, 7th August 1914.

14. See also Hamilton, op. cit., pp. 69-72. Beware of Hamilton's patronising attitude towards the British army of 1914 and its senior officers in particular.

15. 2/Seaforth, War Diary, 9th August 1914. PRO: W095/1483.

16. Haldane, *A Brigade of the Old Army*, p.5. Capt. T.H.C. Frankland added this appendix to the *War Diaries* of 2/R. Dublin Fusiliers: "The weight of the web equipment together with the contents of pack, haversack, & 120 rounds [of] ammunition was found to be so great that many men were physically incapable of carrying it. After a long march the weight tells, especially on the shoulders.

Great difficulty was experienced in impressing on reservists the necessity of the equipment fitting correctly, and many of them afterwards suffered from this.

Many reservists boots were badly fitted & had to be cut before they could get them on. This was, I think, due to the measurements which were taken when they went to the reserve being incorrect." PRO: W095/1481. (The total weight carried by a British infantryman in 1914 was 59lbs 6 3/4 ozs, made up of the clothing worn, rifle and bayonet, 120 rounds of ammunition, entrenching tool and carrier, web equipment [including water bottle and contents], the pack and its contents, iron rations and the "unexpired portion" of the day's ration. Any personal items carried were in addition to this load. P.T.S.)

17. Hamilton, op. cit., p.72.

18. Hill, op. cit., p.10

19. Snow, op. cit., p.8.

20. The *Caledonia* disembarked not only the troops, but also a sailor who deserted the ship, following the example of three others who had deserted at Havre during the night of 14/15th August. Apparently this problem was common to many of the vessels transporting the BEF.

21. Haldane was apparently under the impression that part of his brigade had landed at Havre (*A Brigade of the Old Army*, p.10), but in fact all of it landed at Boulogne. The 4th Division was divided between Havre, Rouen and Boulogne.

22. Napoleon's Column, built to commemorate the assembly of his army (172,000 infantry and 9,000 cavalry) to invade England in 1804.

Chapter 3 (pages 18-23)

1. *Military Operations: France and Belgium, 1914.* [Vol. 1]. Compiled by Br.-Gen. Sir James E. Edmonds. (Macmillan, 1933) p.49.

2. Sir Horace Smith-Dorrien had been sent to replace the original commander of II Corps, Lt.-Gen. Sir James Grierson, who had died suddenly aboard the train carrying him to his headquarters.

3. Smith-Dorrien (Gen. Sir Horace) *[Typescript diary]*, 23rd August 1914. PRO: CAB45/206.

4. *Military Operations*, p.90.

5. *Military Operations*, p.93.

6. In his typescript diary, 24th August 1914, Smith-Dorrien gives the time of receipt as 2am.

7. Williamson, op. cit, p.366.

8. Smith-Dorrien (Gen. Sir Horace) *Statement with regard to Lord French's Book "1914"* p.17.

9. Smith-Dorrien, ibid, p.15.

10. Smith-Dorrien, ibid, p.16; *Military Operations*, p.97, gives the time of receipt as 2am.

11. Smith-Dorrien, *Statement*, p.14 *Military Operations*, p. 98, gives the time of the meeting between Smith-Dorrien and Haig as about 12 noon on 24th August 1914.

12. Smith-Dorrien, *Typescript diary*, 24th August 1914.

13. *Military Operations*, p.99.

14. Smith Dorrien, *Statement*, p.16.

15. *Military Operations*, p.99.

16. ibid, p.101

17. ibid, p.112

18. ibid, p.114
19. Smith-Dorrien, *Typescript diary*, 24th August 1914.
20. Smith Dorrien, *Statement*, p.21.
21. ibid, pp.21-22
22. *Military Operations*, p.120

Chapter 4 (pages 24-29)

1. 4th Division, General Staff, War Diary, 23rd August 1914. PRO: W095/1439.
2. Snow, op. cit, p.11.
3. Snow, op. cit, p.11. My emphasis.
4. Snow, op. cit, pp.11-12. As regards impressed labour, on 24th August 1914 Captain H.C. Hart (1/R. Warwickshire) certainly saw "a squad of peasants, men in their blue blouses, shouldering their long handled spades, returning or on their way to dig trenches." PRO: CAB45/196.
5. *Military Operations*, pp.147-148. The 4th Division's original mounted troops were B Sqdn., 19th Hussars, but they were withdrawn to help form a composite Cavalry Regiment and replaced by what turned out to be only half of A Sqdn., North Irish Horse. They lost touch with the 4th Division and fought instead with the 3rd Division until late on 28th August.
6. Hill, op. cit., p.11.
7. Hart (Capt. H.C.) *Narrative of Retreat from Mons: 1st Battalion Royal Warwickshire Regiment*, 24th August 1914. PRO: CAB45/196.
8. Hill, op. cit., p.11.
9. Clarke (Capt. N.P.) "Through German Lines" in *Blackwood's Magazine*, (June, 1915) p.717-718.
10. Mainwaring (Lt.-Col. A.E.) *A Statement*, p.1.
11. Clarke, op.cit., p.719.
12. Capt. Cyril Walter Carleton Wasey, MC. Killed in action 28/10/17.
13. Haldane, *A Brigade of the Old Army*, p.14.
14. 4th Division, General Staff, War Diary, 25th August 1914.
15. Hart, op.cit., 25th August 1914.
16. Hart, op.cit., 25th August 1914.
17. Montgomery (Field-Marshal The Viscount) "Diary kept by Lt. ... B.L. Montgomery..." in *The Antelope*, vol. 14, 1938, p.67.
18. Haldane, *A Brigade of the Old Army*, p.15.
19. Mainwaring, op. cit., p.2.
20. Clarke, op. cit., p.720.
21. Hart, op. cit., 25th August 1914.

Chapter 5 (pages 30-35)

1. *Military Operations*, p.124.
2. ibid, p.141.
3. Smith-Dorrien, *Statement*, p.34.
4. ibid, p.36.
5. Maj. Basil Walcot, DSO, RE. Died 14/9/18.
6. *Military Operations*, p.135.
7. ibid, p.142.

8. Hart, op. cit., 25th August 1914.
9. ibid, 25th August 1914.
10. Snow, op. cit., p.16.
11. Haldane, *A Brigade of the Old Army*, p.17.
12. Clarke, op. cit., p.721.
13. Haldane, *A Brigade of the Old Army*, p.19.
14. *Military Operations*, p.147.
15. 4th Division, General Staff, War Diary, app. "Action of Ligny Haucout," p.3.
16. Snow, op. cit., p.17.
17. ibid
18. *Military Operations*, p.149.

Chapter 6 (pages 36-42)

1. 2/Seaforth Highlanders, War Diary, 26th August 1914. PRO: W095/1483.
2. Hart, op.cit., 26th August 1914.
3. ibid.
4. Macky (2/Lt. F.C.S.) PRO: CAB 45/197.
5. No two accounts agree precisely on the relative positions of the 1/R. Warwickshire and 2/R. Dublin Fusiliers, but the majority place the Dublins to the right of the Warwickshire.
6. Mainwaring, op.cit., p.2.
7. Clarke, op.cit. p.721.
8. Hart, op.cit., 26th August 1914.
9. *Military Operations*, p.165.
10. These were probably the batteries of the horse artillery *abteilung* of *Feld-Artillerie Regiment 35* of the 2. *Kavallerie-Division*. Each battery was equipped with four 7.7-cm *Feldkanone*. If all three batteries were in action simultaneously the effect of the concentrated fire of all twelve guns for twenty minutes can only be imagined.
11. Hart, op.cit., 26th August 1914.
12. According to *Military Operations* the attack by two companies of the Warwickshire "from the reserve" was made "by direction of a staff officer." (p. 165). *Military Operations* also mentions a second attack by two companies of Warwickshire at about 8.45am. This is not mentioned in the Warwickshire records. Captain Hart's account mentions that a company of the Dublin Fusiliers joined the Warwickshire's attack to assist the King's Own. It is not mentioned in the Dublin's War Diary or in any of their personal accounts except that of Captain Clarke who was commanding A Coy. in the front line:"...I met a staff officer belonging to the brigade on our right [11th Brigade] who said: "They are very hard pushed on that ridge, and my brigadier wants support. The right of your brigade are going to reinforce. Can't you take up your company?" Telling him I would see if I could, I hurried across to the second in command [Major H.M. Shewan] and gave him the message. He gave me leave to take up my company, and said the other front company would come forward to hold my trenches and give us covering fire in case we need it.

My company then rapidly advanced... The enemy got the ridge before we could reach it, and drove our advanced troops off it. So the company was ordered to retire, and came back to its original positiion with the loss of two wounded." *Blackwood's Magazine*, June 1915, p.722.

13. Montgomery, *Memoirs*, p.32.

14. Major William Charles Christie. Killed in action 13/10/14.

15. Hart, op. cit., 26th August 1914.

16. Montgomery, "Diary," p.67. Captain Hart recalled: "In the course of the morning the stretcher bearers, being unmolested by the enemy, collected all our wounded and removed them either to Ligny or Haucourt, but as we had no ambulances, only a few were evacuated from these places, however, a lucky few were got away in country carts; the others subsequently fell into the enemy's hands." PRO: CAB45/196.

17. Hamilton, op. cit., p.76.

18. See note 5, above.

19. Mainwaring, op. cit., p.2. Lt.-Col. Hugh Mackenzie Shewan, DSO (1870-?).

20. Lt.-Col. Norman Percy Clarke (1878-?). Major Gordon Shakespeare Higginson (1874-?).

21. Mainwaring, op. cit., p.2.

22. The third battery of XXXII Brigade, no. 135, was placed in close defence of Ligny.

23. Mainwaring, op. cit, p.3.

24. Lt.-Col. Henry Irving Rodney Allfrey, Somerset Light Infantry, DSO, MC (1879-?).

25. Lt.-Gen. Sir Basil Ferguson Burnett-Hitchcock, KCB, DSO (1877-1938).

26. Mainwaring, op, cit, p.3.

Chapter 7 (pages 43-48)

1. Hart, op.cit., 26th August 1914.

2. *Military Operations*, p. 184.

3. Mainwaring, op, cit, p.3.

4. Burrowes (Maj. A.R.) *Private Diary*, 26th August 1914. PRO WO95/1482. Br.-Gen. Arnold Robinson Burrowes, CMG, DSO (1867-1949). Noted in *Who's Who* as the "designer of the service web equipment worn throughout the army."

5. Becke (Maj. A.F.) *The Royal Regiment of Artillery at Le Cateau, Wednesday, 26th August 1914* (Royal Artillery Institution, 1919) p.53.

6. ibid, p.65.

7. Mainwaring, op, cit, p.3.

8. ibid, p.3.

9. ibid, p.4.

10. Watson (Capt. R.M.) PRO: WO95/1477 and 1481.

11. Mainwaring, op, cit, p.4.

12. Watson, op.cit.

13. Major A.J. Poole estimated the total as 350 of all regiments. PRO: W095/1484.

14. Hart, op.cit., 26th August 1914.

15. Br.-Gen Arthur James Poole, CB, CMG (1872-1956)

16. Hart, op.cit., 26th August 1914.

17. Poole (Maj. A.J.) PRO: W095/1484

18. See Hart and Clarke for conflicting accounts of the German occupation of Haucourt. It is said that the British wounded remained in the village for five days and were tended by the local curé and members of his flock who scoured the battlefield for abandoned emergency rations to feed them. The priest also extended his help to unwounded British soldiers in hiding and he was later arrested by the Germans, condemned to death and shot.

19. Clarke, op, cit., p.725.

20. Hart, op.cit., 26th August 1914.

21. ibid.

22. Clarke, op.cit., 26th August 1914.

23. ibid.

24. Hart, op.cit., 26th August 1914.

25. Hart, op.cit., 26th August 1914. They met a small party of the missing North Irish Horse in Caullery. See Chapter 4, Note 5.

26. Cowper (Col. J.M.) *The King's Own: The Story of a Royal Regiment.* Vol. III. (Gale and Polden, 1957) p.15.

27. Macky (2/Lt. F.C.S.) PRO: CAB45/197.

28. Clarke, op. cit., p. 727.

Chapter 8 (pages 49-54)

1. Frankland (Capt. T.H.C.) PRO: W095/1477

2. ibid.

3. Mainwaring, op.cit., p.4.

4. Frankland, op.cit.

5. Mainwaring, op.cit., p.4.

6. Lt.-Col. Francis Edward Lloyd Daniell, DSO, Seaforth Highlanders. Died of wounds 4/3/16.

7. Lt. C.P. Cowper, Royal Warwickshire, Special Reserve.

8. Mainwaring, op.cit., pp.4-5.

9. The Director of Railway Transport at this date was Col. J.H. Twiss. Maj. D.S. MacInnes, DSO, was GSO2 at the Headquarters, Lines of Communication Defences.

10. Smith-Dorrien, *Statement*, p.50

11. Coleman (Frederic) *From Mons to Ypres with French* (Samson Low, Marston, 1916) p.28.

There are two other accounts by volunteer drivers, *From Chauffeur to Brigadier* by Br.-Gen. C.B. Baker-Carr (Benn, 1930) and *Adventures on the Western Front, August, 1914 - June 1915* by [Lt.-Col.] A. Rawlinson (Melrose, 1925). In an appendix to the GHQ War Diary dated 23rd August 1914 it was noted: "Several of the cars brought by the specially enlisted M.T. drivers were found to be unsuitable and had to be returned; none came provided with spares and tools, which were indispensable to active service conditions." WO95/1.

12. Deedes (General Sir Charles) "The View from G.H.Q.," Pt. 2. In *Stand To! The Journal of the Western Front Association.* No. 11. Summer, 1984. p.11.

13. Coleman, op.cit., p.28.

14. ibid. p.34.

15. Smith-Dorrien does not mention this meeting in his diary or *Statement*.

16. This is presumed to be Br.-Gen. P.E.F. Hobbs, CMG, DA & QMG I Corps. It is not clear why he was in the II Corps area.

17. Osburn (see below) mentions "one or two pale exhausted-looking subalterns whom I noticed mingling with the crowd down at the station". Other than Lt. C.P. Cowper (see note 7 above) the officers have yet to be identified.

18. Mainwaring, op.cit., pp.5-7.

Chapter 9 (pages 55-59)

1. Lt.-Gen. Sir G. Tom M. Bridges, KCB, KCMG, DSO (1871-1939).

2. Bridges (Lt.-Gen. Sir Tom) *Alarms and Excursions* (Longmans Green 1938) pp.85-86.

3. Gibb (Rev. Harold) *Record of the 4th Royal Irish Dragoon Guards in the Great War, 1914-1918* (Canterbury, 1925) p.11.

4. Osburn (Arthur) *Unwilling Passenger* (Faber & Faber, 1932) p.78. Lt.-Col. Arthur Carr Osburn, DSO, RAMC (1876-1952).

5. Bridges, op.cit., p.86.

6. ibid.

7. Br.-Gen. Horace Somerville Sewell, CMG, DSO and bar (1881-1953).

8. Bridges, op.cit., p.86.

9. Mainwaring, op.cit., p.7. It is not known when or why Elkington left, nor where he went.

10. Bridges, op.cit., p.87.

11. ibid.

12. Osburn, op.cit., p.79. His italics.

13. ibid, p.86.

14. Mainwaring, op.cit., p.7.

15. Osburn, op.cit., p.83.

16. ibid, pp.87-88. Bridges and his impromptu band became the subject of a poem, "The Toy Band (A Song of the Great Retreat)," by Sir Henry Newbolt.

17. Mainwaring, op.cit., pp.7-8.

18. ibid., p.8.

19. Osburn, op.cit., pp.83-84

20. ibid, p.85.

21. ibid, p.85.

22. On 28th August St. Quentin was occupied by *Genmaj.* Fleck's *14.Inf.Div. (VII Armeekorps, 2. Armee).*

Chapter 10 (pages 60-68)

1. Clarke, op.cit., p. 728. His emphasis.

2. In each infantry battalion nine signallers were provided with bicycles.

3. Clarke, op.cit., p.730.

4. ibid, p.731.

5. ibid, p.734.

6. ibid, p.735.

7. ibid, p.740.

8. ibid, p.p.745-746.

9. ibid, p.p.746-747.

10. The story of the surrender of the 1/Gordon Highlanders (8th Bde., 3rd Division) at Le Cateau and its aftermath is best told by Dr. A.J. Peacock in "A Serious Misfortune: The 1st Gordon Highlanders in August 1914." In *Gun Fire: A Journal of First World War History.* No.22. York, n.d.

11. Clarke, op.cit., p.750.

12. ibid, p.752.

13. ibid, p.753.

14. ibid.

15. ibid, p.p.753-754.

16. Hart, op.cit., p.10. According to *Military Operations* (p.196) Poole was joined at Caullery at dawn "by another platoon of the Dublin Fusiliers under Lieutenant R.F.H. Massy-Westropp, who had retired at dusk from his trenches in the road between Ligny and Haucourt and, finding his retreat threatened by a party of Germans in a farm, had promptly attacked them, driven them away and gone on his way unmolested."

17. Hart, op.cit., 27th August 1914. See note 10 above.

18. Poole (Maj. A.J.) PRO: WO95/1477. According to Capt. Hart "the machine gunners were unable any longer to draw their guns which they had placed in a kind of hand truck; the guns were therefore buried." 27th August 1914. PRO: CAB45/196.

19. The surviving machine-gun of the 1/King's Own was dumped down a well in Haucourt by the machine-gun officer, Lt. L.S. Woodgate.

20. Hart, op.cit., 27th August 1914.

21. ibid.

22. ibid, 28th August 1914.

23. ibid.

24. ibid.

25. ibid, 29th August 1914.

26. Montgomery, *The Memoirs* p.32.

Chapter 11 (pages 69-73)

1. Br.-Gen. Sir Gilbert Mellor, KBE, CB, CMG (1872-1947).

2. *The Times* (various dates); Commonwealth War Graves Commission; Andy Simpson.

Sources
Unpublished

Anonymous. Account of 1/East Lancashire, 1914. IWM Misc. 154(2388).

Burrowes (Maj. A.R.) PRO W095/1482.

Churcher (Lt.-Col. D.W.) PRO WO95/1482.

Frankland (Capt. T.H.C.) PRO WO95/1477.

French (Field-Marshal Sir John) PRO WO95/1.

Haldane (Br.-Gen. J.A.L.) Typescript copy of diary for 28 April 1912-7 August 1914 [Shorncliffe diary]. IWM 69/36/1.

Hart (Capt. H.C.) PRO CAB45/196.

Kavanagh (Capt. V.H.) PRO W095/1482.

Knight-Bruce (Lt. J.H.W.) PRO CAB45/196.
Macky (2/Lt. F.C.S.) PRO CAB45/197.
Poole (Maj. A.J.) PRO WO95/1477.
Smith-Dorrien (General Sir Horace) PRO CAB45/206.
Snow (Maj.-Gen. T. D'O.) PRO CAB45/129.
Watson (Capt. R.M.) PRO WO95/1477 and 1481.
West (Lt. C.H. L'E.) PRO CAB45/197.
Wheeler (Capt. S.G. de C.) PRO/1477.
General Headquarters, Section O(B), General Staff. War Diary. PRO W095/1.
4th Division, General Staff. War Diary. PRO WO95/1439.
4th Division, Adjutant & Quarter-Master General. PRO WO95/1449.
10th Infantry Brigade, Headquarters. War Diary. PRO WO95/1477.
1/R. Warwickshire. War Diary. PRO WO95/1484.
2/R. Dublin Fusiliers. War Diary. PRO WO95/1482.
1/R. Irish Fusiliers. War Diary. PRO WO95/1482.
2/Seaforth Highlanders. War Diary PRO WO95/1483.

Published

My thanks are due to the authors and publishers of the following works which have been a great assistance in the preparation of this work.

Baker-Carr (Br.-Gen. C.B.) *From Chauffeur to Brigadier.* Benn, 1930.
Battle of Le Cateau, 26th August, 1914: Tour of the Battlefield. HMSO, 1934.
Becke (Maj. A.F.) *The Royal Regiment of Artillery at Le Cateau, Wednesday, 26th August, 1914.* Royal Artillery Institution, Woolwich, 1919.
Beckett (Dr. Ian F.W.). *The Judgement of History: Sir Horace Smith-Dorrien, Lord French and "1914."* Tom Donovan, 1993. (Incorporates Gen. Sir Horace Smith-Dorrien's *Statement with regard to the first edition of Lord French's book "1914"*).
Bloem (Walter). *The Advance from Mons 1914.* Award Books, New York and Tandem Books, London, 1967. (Originally published in 1930).
Bridges (Br.-Gen. Sir Tom). *Alarms & Excursions: Reminiscences of a Soldier.* Longmans Green, 1938.
Burrowes (Br.-Gen. A.R.) *The 1st Battalion The Faugh-A-Ballaghs [Royal Irish Fusiliers] in the Great War.* Gale & Polden, Aldershot, [1925].
Caffrey (Kate). *Farewell, Leicester Square: The Old Contemptibles 12 August - 19 November 1914.* Andre Deutsch, 1980.
Clarke (Capt. N.P.). "Through the German Lines." In *Blackwood's Magazine.* June, 1915.
Coleman (Frederic). *From Mons to Ypres with French; a personal narrative.* Sampson Low, Marston, 1916.
Cowper (Col. J.M.) *The King's Own: The Story of a Royal Regiment.* Vol.III: *1914-1950.* Gale & Poulden, Aldershot, 1957.
Deedes (General Sir Charles). "The View from G.H.Q." Pt. 2. In *Stand To! The Journal of the Western Front Association.* No. 11. Summer, 1984.
Edmonds (Br.-Gen. Sir James E.) compiler. *Military Operations: France and*

Belgium, 1914. (Vol. 1). Macmillan, 1933. Third Ed., revised. (Official History).

Elkington (A.E.H.) & (C.M.). *The Elkingtons of Bath.* [Woodstock, 1959].

Field Service Manual, 1914: Infantry Battalion (Expeditionary Force). HMSO, 1914.

Finley (R. Mainwaring). *A Short History of the Mainwaring Family.* Research Publishing, 1976. (Facsimile reprint of the original edition of 1890).

Gibb (Rev. Harold). *Record of the 4th Royal Irish Dragoon Guards in the Great War, 1914-1918.* Canterbury, 1925.

Haldane (Gen. Sir Aylmer). *A Brigade of the Old Army 1914.* Arnold, 1920.

—*A Soldier's Saga: The Autobiography.* Wm. Blackwood & Sons, 1948.

Hamilton (Nigel). *Monty: The Making of a General 1887-1942.* Hamish Hamilton, 1981.

Hazlehurst (Cameron). *Polticians at War, July 1914 to May 1915.* Cape, 1971.

Hill (R.G.). "An Old Contemptible at Le Cateau." In *Everyman at War: Sixty Personal Narratives of the War.* Ed. by C.B. Purdom. Dent, 1930.

Kingsford (C.L.) *The Story of the Royal Warwickshire Regiment.* "Country Life", [1921].

Macdonald (Lyn). *1914.* Michael Joseph, 1987.

Mainwaring (Lt.-Col. A.E.) *A Statement* [by] *A.E.M.* N.p.,N.d.

Montgomery (Field Marshal The Viscount). *The Memoirs.* Collins, 1958.

—Diary Kept by Lt. (now Brig.) B.L. Montgomery, "C" Coy., 1st Bn. R.War.R. From 22nd August to 18th October, 1914." In *The Antelope.* Vol. 14. 1938.

Osburn (Arthur). *Unwilling Passenger.* Faber & Faber, 1932.

Peacock (Dr. A.J.). "A Serious Misfortune: The 1st Gordon Highlanders in August 1914." In *Gun Fire.* No. 22. York, n.d.

Poinsot (M.-C.). *Les Volontaires Étrangers de 1914.* Dorbon-Ainé, Paris, 1915.

Porch (Douglas). *The French Foreign Legion: A Complete History.* Macmillan, 1991.

Rawlinson ([Lt.-Col.] A.). *Adventures on the Western Front, August 1914-June 1915.* Andrew Melrose. 1915.

Romer (Major C.F.) and Mainwaring (Major A.E.). *The Second Battalion Royal Dublin Fusiliers in the South African War.* Arthur L. Humphreys, 1908.

Scott (Peter T.) "Mobilization 1914." In *War Monthly.* Vol. 7, No. 67. August, 1979.

Sym (Colonel John) ed. *Seaforth Highlanders.* Gale & Polden, Aldershot, 1962.

Terraine (John). *Mons: The Retreat to Victory.* Batsford, 1960.

The Times. Various dates.

War Establishments. Part I. Expeditionary Force 1914. HMSO, 1914.

Der Weltkrieg 1914 bis 1918: Die militarischen Operationen zu Lande. Erster Band: *Die Grenzschlachten im Westen.* Bearbeitet im Reichsarchiv. Mittler, Berlin, 1925.

Williamson (Samuel R.). *The Politics of Grand Strategy: Britain and France Prepare for War, 1904-1914.* Harvard Universty Press, Cambridge, Mass., 1969.

Wylly (Col. H.C.). *Crown and Company: The Historical Records of the 2nd Battalion Royal Dublin Fusiliers.* Vol.2: 1911-1922. G&P, Aldershot, [1923].